A NATIONAL
on th
PERMANENT DIACONATE
OF THE CATHOLIC CHURCH
IN THE UNITED STATES

....

1 9 9 4 - 1 9 9 5

On September 14, 1993, the Administrative Committee of the National Conference of Catholic Bishops approved a proposal from the Committee on the Permanent Diaconate to undertake a two-year, four-phase study of the Permanent Diaconate in the United States. In its planning document, as approved by the general membership of the National Conference of Catholic Bishops in November 1993, the Committee on the Permanent Diaconate was authorized to undertake this study. Brought to completion, this final report of the study, approved by the chairman and members of the Committee on the Permanent Diaconate, is authorized for publication by the undersigned.

Monsignor Dennis M. Schnurr
General Secretary
NCCB/USCC

ISBN 1-55586-087-7

Contents

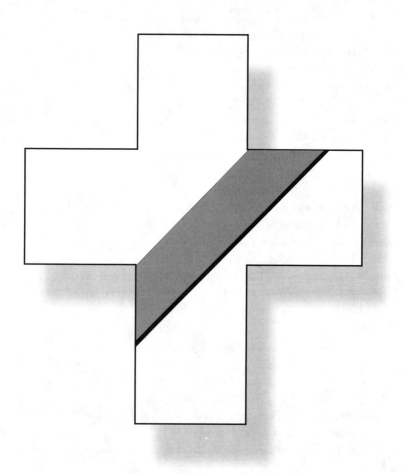

Acknowledgments

We are indebted to Reverend Eugene F. Hemrick, director of research for the National Conference of Catholic Bishops, Doctor James R. Kelly, professor of sociology at Fordham University, and Deacon Samuel M. Taub, executive director of the NCCB Secretariat for the Diaconate, who were responsible for the formulation of the study and the preparation of the final report.

Special thanks are due to Bishop Dale J. Melczek who generously accepted the responsibility to serve as manager for this project.

We are most grateful to the members of the National Conference of Catholic Bishops and the Catholic Church Extension Society of the United States of America for the funding of the National Study project, without which the study could not have been undertaken.

Thanks are given to Dorothy Kane, Mary Ann Eley, Ann Kasprzyk, Amy Kochel, Mei-Chu Lin, Fengang Yang, and Yang Su of the Center for Studies in Religion and Culture at The Catholic University of America, who were responsible for the data processing; and Dottie Titman and Theresa Spinner, who assembled and prepared the final text.

Acknowledgment is made with gratitude for the encouragement, advice, and practical assistance provided by Sister Sharon Euart, RSM, NCCB associate general secretary, and (now) Bishop Robert N. Lynch, former NCCB general secretary, both of whom helped to bring this project to fruition.

Foreword

During his pastoral visit to the Church in the United States in 1987, Pope John Paul II addressed the deacons of our country. The Holy Father told the deacons, ". . . you represent a great and visible sign of the working of the Holy Spirit . . . I give thanks to God for the call you have received and for your generous response." The response to which the Holy Father referred has been an uninterrupted growth of the diaconate in the United States. The year 1994 marked the twenty-fifth anniversary of the restoration and renewal of the diaconate as a permanent order in the Church, open to both married and celibate men. Today deacons number more than eleven thousand, nearly twice the number of deacons in the rest of the Universal Church combined—a sign, indeed, of the working of the Holy Spirit.

During June 1986, at Saint John's Abbey in Collegeville, Minnesota, the National Conference of Catholic Bishops met in a special assembly to consider vocations and future church leadership. In a presentation on the ordained ministry, Archbishop Daniel Pilarczyk said, "Unlike other ministers, it is clear that we are not dealing with dearth in the permanent diaconate but with abundance. I believe that we do not yet know what that abundance means." In summarizing the ten days of discussion, Cardinal Joseph Bernardin, referring to the discussion on the diaconate, said, "While the experience of many is positive, a number of concerns were voiced. These include the identity of the deacon, his effective incorporation into the pastoral ministries of the diocese and its parishes, a danger of elitism and clericalism, the need for better screening and training. In light of the comments made, I am convinced that we should seriously evaluate our experience. Such a study would be helpful in determining future directions."

At the fall 1992 meeting of the National Conference of Catholic Bishops' Administrative Committee and during the plenary meeting of the Conference that same fall, Archbishop Patrick F. Flores, then chair-

man of the bishops' Committee on the Permanent Diaconate, present-
ed a summary report on the diaconate as a means of providing an
account of his stewardship during his three-year tenure as chairman.
Both presentations stimulated questions about the diaconate that
reflected those enumerated by both Archbishop Pilarczyk and Cardinal
Bernardin seven years earlier. Thus it appeared that there were even
more urgent reasons to consider undertaking the study about which
Cardinal Bernardin spoke with conviction in 1986.

A proposal to undertake a four-phase, two-year study of the diaconate in the United States was approved by the Conference. Funding
was secured from the National Conference of Catholic Bishops and the
Catholic Church Extension Society of the United States of America.

Over the course of two years, data were assembled based on the
experience of deacons (Phase I), the wives of deacons (Phase II), the
supervisors of deacons in ministry (Phase III), and parish and diocesan
lay leaders (Phase IV).

The study project was initiated on January 2, 1994. The chairman
of the bishops' Committee on the Diaconate, Bishop Dale J. Melczek,
generously undertook the responsibility to organize and manage the
study. He was ably assisted by members of the committee; the director
of the Conference's Office of Research, Reverend Eugene Hemrick;
Dr. James R. Kelly, Department of Sociology, Fordham University; and
executive director of the Conference's Secretariat for the Diaconate,
Deacon Samuel M. Taub.

In December 1995, a summary report which included an analysis
of the findings of this study, conclusions drawn from the data, and
issues for the future, was published and distributed to the bishops of
the Conference and diocesan directors of the diaconate.

While this activity was under way in the United States, the Holy
Father authorized the Congregation for the Clergy to devote its fall
1995 plenary assembly to the permanent diaconate. In advance of this,
on December 16, 1993, the prefect of the Congregation, Cardinal José

Sanchez, sent all diocesan bishops a ten-question instrument to gather worldwide data on the criteria for selection of men for the diaconate; their formation; the apostolates in which deacons were engaged; relationships with bishops, priests, and the laity; theological, juridic, pastoral, and financial "problems" encountered; and structures and policy statements on the diaconate.

The Congregation for the Clergy *plenarium* was held from November 28 through December 1, 1995. Three deacons were invited —from the United States, Europe, and Latin America—to address the Fathers of the *plenaria* on the experience of the diaconate in the particular churches of those continents. Upon completion of their work, in the Sala Clementina of the Apostolic Palace, the Holy Father addressed the participants in the *plenarium*. He thanked them for their efforts and their intention to prepare a document concerning the life and ministry of deacons that would be similar to that for priests, which the members of the Congregation addressed in their preceding plenary session. The Holy Father foresaw that "it will be possible to offer *providential practical guidance* following the Second Vatican Council's decisions (i.e., to restore and renew the diaconate). . . . I encourage and bless your efforts, motivated as they are by a deep love for the Church and for our brother deacons."

As we await the publication of the document of the Holy See devoted to the diaconate, we now publish the final report of our two-year study, with the hope that these two documents will provide the firm foundation for (1) the revision of our *Guidelines* for the formation and ministry of deacons, and (2) the determination by the National Conference of Catholic Bishops, under the guidance of the Holy Spirit, of future directions for this servant ministry in the Third Millennium, at the threshold of which we now stand.

MOST REVEREND EDWARD U. KMIEC
Chairman
Bishops' Committee on the Diaconate

FACING THE CHALLENGES
OF SUCCESS

· · · · · · · · · · · · · · · · ·

A National Survey of the

Order of the Diaconate in the United States

Introduction

A summary of the four national surveys of deacons, deacons' wives, supervisors/directors of deacons, and parish lay leaders should begin with its central finding: The restored order of the diaconate has been hugely successful, and, as Table 1 reflects, it is growing at a steady rate (see Appendix A).[1] The vast majority of deacons themselves said they were ready to advise others to pursue this ministry. These data corroborate and extend the findings of an early national study of the diaconate,[2] which also reported high satisfaction. The data show some disappointments but contain no disillusionment. Their supervisors described the deacons' largely parish-based ministries as successful and increasingly important for the life of the Church. Lay leaders reported widespread and enthusiastic acceptance of the ministries performed by deacons. Fifty-nine percent of the lay leaders (with no difference between men and women) in our sample answered "very positive" and another 35 percent said "positive" to the direct question, "In 1968 the permanent diaconate was restored in the U.S. From what you have observed of all permanent deacons who have served in the parish, what is your general reaction to the restoration of the diaconate?"

Deacons' wives described themselves as supportive of their husband's ministry and their family as greatly enriched by his ordination and service.

While the deacons, their wives, and their supervisors described problems of deacon identity and acceptance, they reported them in the larger context of high satisfaction and characterized them as remediable by better communication and personal relations (see Tables 2 and 3).

Parish lay leaders were the least likely to perceive problems of deacon identity or of collaboration among deacons, priests, and lay staff. The great majority of parish leaders foresaw a growth in the diaconate. A large number explicitly analyzed the future of the diaconate in the context of the declining number of parish priests.

From the data gathered by our four national samples[3] we might characterize the primary challenge of the diaconate for the future as the challenge to broaden its ministries beyond its largely successful and increasingly indispensable adaption to parish life. The 1981 study found that while a majority of the deacons thought of themselves in "traditional roles" (liturgical activities and proclaiming the Word), about one-third and one-fifth, respectively, based their deacons' identities more on ministries of counseling and of social action. During the post-1981 period it appears that this pluralism of ministries did not continue to evolve.

Who Are the Deacons?

While the deacons range in age from 40 to 86, their average (and median) age is almost 60.[4] In the 1981 study, the median age was 49 (see Figure 1). Sixty percent reported professional or managerial careers that usually followed at least a college education. These are higher levels of education than the already high levels reported in the 1981 study.

Only 3 percent were never married (the 1981 study found 7%), and about 18 percent reported "minority" backgrounds (about one-half of these use a self-identification of "Hispanic-Latino"). Since 1981, there has been only a slight increase in the percentages of non-Caucasian deacons: from 3 to 4 percent African American and from 9 to 10 percent Hispanic-Latino. The number of Asian and Native American deacons has also increased only slightly.

While a little over one-half the deacons said that at one time they had considered the priesthood, only about one-third asserted that this earlier consideration was at least a strong influence on their becoming a deacon. They described the "need to deepen the service(s) I was already giving to the Church" as more proximate and far stronger. The deacons' wives agreed. Very few "feel that my husband really wishes he had pursued ordination to the priesthood." Their wives reported that they also were highly active in the Church both before and after their husband's ordination.

Family Life and Diaconal Responsibilities

The deacons mostly felt that their ministry has enriched their family, their relationship with their wife, and their home life; although the write-in comments sometimes distinguished the experience of ministry when children are younger as different from when they are older. In fact, the great majority of the deacons have completed their child-rearing responsibilities. In the aggregate, the deacons average fewer than one child still living at home. Their wives, their supervisors, and lay leaders in the parishes to which deacons are assigned corroborated the deacons' judgment that their ministry and their diaconal responsibilities have been complementary rather than competitive. When asked if the deacons' ministerial duties ever conflicted with their family obligations, one-third of their supervisors answered "never" and another one-half said "sometimes." Most (71%) lay leaders perceived no large problem for deacons in balancing their family and ministerial responsibilities. Women lay leaders were only slightly more likely than men to perceive difficulties arising from deacon family obligations. About one-third of lay leaders answered that "sometimes" they saw conflicts, but an equal percentage said "never or rarely." Only 1 percent of the wives (6% were not sure) said that if they "knew then what they know now" they would not consent to their husband's ordination.

The great majority of the wives felt involved in their husband's training and continued to feel part of his ministry. Indeed, most of the wives said that they had their own parish ministries. Many noted in their write-in comments that during their formation programs, the deacons were taught "family first, job second, diaconate third." These norms seem to be shared implicitly by parishioners as well.

Only 6 percent of the wives felt "the parish expects too much of me because of my husband's position as a deacon." About as few said they "sometimes feel that I am in competition with the Church for my husband's love and affection." Two-thirds said they never have felt the need for a support group to better understand their husband's ministry, although quite a few recommended more "preparation days" for the wives of men in formation, given by wives whose husbands had been ordained for at least five years.

The write-in comments show that as a result of being a part of the diaconate, the couple had more enriching experiences, met more people and on deeper levels, and had more to share and talk about. Both said the diaconate has brought them human and spiritual growth. On this point, our findings simply confirm the 1981 findings. They too found high deacon and spouse satisfaction, and that only 2 percent of the deacons said their ministry had weakened their marriage relationship. In both studies, almost all the wives strongly agreed with their husband's appraisal.[5]

What Do Deacons Do?
What Will They Do?

Deacons do many things, but the data suggest they mostly do the things that priests did unaided before the restoration of the diaconate. Apparently this is what most deacons thought they *would be doing*. Most say that their initial vision of the diaconate has been fulfilled. From the start, two-thirds anticipated that they would serve in their home parish where, in fact, most did their field work. Most currently serve in largely liturgical and sacramental roles, and they perform these expected tasks quite well. According to their supervisors (who are mostly the pastors of the parishes where the deacons serve), they ably perform these duties. Almost all of their supervisors (95%, 58% of which added "very") described the deacons' work in sacramental activities such as baptisms, marriages, and liturgies as effective (see Table 4). While their supervisors rated all other deacon roles as effective, the majority added "very" only to two others—pastoral care of the sick and giving homilies. Roles receiving the lowest number (less than 20%) of "very effective" ratings were the less traditional ones such as prison ministries, promoting human and civil rights, and working with small base communities. Between the highly effective and lesser effective roles were (in order) the following: religious education; work with the poor; RCIA; "preach, teach, or inform others about the social teaching of the Church"; evangelization; counseling; parish/diocesan administration; leader of a prayer group; marriage encounter; charismatic renewal; and involvement in pro-life activities.

When asked about the effectiveness of the deacons in their ministries, parish lay leaders gave answers strikingly similar to the deacons' supervisors. While they rate the deacons' contributions to parish life very highly, they rate deacons as most successful in the more familiar and traditional liturgical and sacramental roles. When asked to evaluate ministries less explicitly tied to the immediate religious needs of parishioners, lay leaders had less knowledge about them and, sensibly, said they had less confidence in evaluating them.

It is worth noting that the amount of preaching done by deacons varies quite a bit. A little more than one-quarter of the lay leaders reported that their deacons "seldom" preached, while another quarter said "very frequently." Lay leaders (47%) perceived that deacons preach "somewhat frequently." The lay leaders (52%) tended to rate deacons' preaching as "about the same in quality" as homilies generally preached by priests. But when they did not judge them as roughly equal, lay leaders were almost twice as likely to rate priests' homilies as higher in quality (31% to 17%).

For the most part, the deacons' directors did not think that these men "would devote the same time to these ministries" if they were not ordained. Only about one-third thought this likely or probable. Fifty-five percent said they did not think the deacons' ministries could be "performed equally well by a lay person without ordination." On the other hand, those answering "probably," "maybe," and "yes definitely" comprised 44 percent of the responses.

Lay leaders were less certain than supervisors about the advantages of ordination. A very slight majority (51%) did not think ordination was necessary for the ministries performed by deacons to be successfully done in their parishes.

While about one-quarter of the supervisors described "the diaconal formation programs with which you are familiar" as not satisfactory (and another 9% said they did not know), most (68%) answered "satisfactory," and 19 percent of these added "very satisfactory." Parish lay leaders are even more confident about the formation programs for their deacons. More than 80 percent of the lay leaders characterized the deacons' formation as adequate (with most of them adding "very"). Not many of them find mistakes in the selection of candidates for ordination. Almost all the lay leaders (94%) affirmed that "if it had been in their power" they "would have agreed to the ordination of the deacon(s) in their parish." Deacons themselves gave the highest overall ratings to their formation programs.

From these data (and, later, the written comments) it appears that the vast majority of supervisors and lay leaders regard their deacons as clearly necessary for their parishes, judge them effective in their parish ministries, and find them satisfactorily trained for these responsibilities. However, both their supervisors and their parish lay leaders are just about evenly divided about whether the deacons' ordination is important for the actual ministries they characterize as ably performed.

We asked the deacons' supervisors and the lay leaders a series of open-ended questions inviting lengthier and more thoughtful responses about the future of the diaconate. Consistent with the fixed-answer survey responses, fewer than a dozen of the hundreds of write-in responses could be interpreted as outright negative about its future. The great majority anticipated a future that was much like the present, differing only because they expect there will be even a greater need for deacons to assist in the parish work in light of an ever-diminishing number of priests. The most common response given by supervisors and lay leaders explicitly referred to a worsening shortage of priests and an increasing reliance on deacons for liturgical and sacramental services. Even the new roles anticipated by the majority—more deacons in parish/diocesan administration—were extensions of the already heavy involvement of deacons as assisting pastors and priests in a parish context.[6]

The data especially clarify that lay leaders have come to view the deacons as essentially an adjunct to the pastor and primarily accountable to him. The 1981 survey reported that only 2 percent of the bishops surveyed "saw the diaconate as a partial answer to the continued shortage of priests." While only a few of the supervisors and directors in our study explicitly welcomed the narrowing of diaconal services to the parish context (the majority simply noted it), the lay leaders showed little evidence of thinking about the diaconate in any context other than the parish. However, among the supervisors and directors there were some clear expressions of ambiguity about this development. More than a few expressed deep concern that the meaning of the diaconate was being misshaped by its de facto absorption into explicitly parish-based clerical roles. A handful of supervisors and lay leaders ventured into issues of broadening the eligibility requirements for ordination.[7]

The most common prediction for the future was the neutrally expressed judgment that there will be fewer priests and more deacons who would increasingly function as "parish administrators," "parish-life coordinators," "parish ministry chaplains," or "satellite-parish leaders." Some, but by no means most, added that they expected a corresponding increase in the number of salaried full-time deacons. Eight percent of the deacons reported that they are already in charge of parish communities lacking a resident pastor.[8] It should be noted that 10.3 percent of parishes in the United States do not have a resident priest.

While some of those expressing a judgment on this prediction were sanguine—noting that the deacons' assumption of administrative work would free pastors for more explicitly priestly work—about three dozen of the supervisors' and directors' responses explicitly described the use of deacons as a pragmatic response to the priest shortage as distorting the meaning of both the priesthood and the diaconate. Some representative comments were: "I'm afraid the diaconate will become more clerical, more liturgical—a stopgap for the priest shortage." "I hope they do not become mini-priests." "I fear deeper confusion with the role of priests and lay people." "We have hundreds of parishioners doing voluntary work. I don't need a liturgy helper." "I hope lay ministry for men and women which is parish based will replace it."

Some of the supervisors—about a dozen—in effect said that the increasing use of deacons in parish administrative roles would lead to a "reconstruction" of the sacrament of orders. Ten persons thought that those deacons with suitable training and personal gifts would be ordained to the priesthood, while another six anticipated the ordination of women to the order of the diaconate. Among lay leaders, about twenty wrote that they expected structural changes in the diaconate. Ten expected deacons to assume all the roles of the priesthood, and nine expected women to enter the diaconate. Almost an equal number anticipated a large increase in deacon-administered parishes with, as one said, "visiting priests available for Mass and confession." In their write-in comments, only three lay leaders mentioned diaconate ministries that were not somehow tied to the future of the priesthood.

Among its conclusions, the 1981 study reported that "deacons are perceived as having their greatest potential in the ministry of charity. Responses to open-ended questions view the deacon as 'a discerner of needs in the marketplace, a bridge between the secular and spiritual.'" By 1995, there were very few of these charity-related responses to open-ended questions about the future of the diaconate.

How Do Deacons Fit In?

Forty-one percent of their supervisors answered "yes" to the question, "Deacons sometimes speak of an 'identity problem.' Is this generally true in your experience?" The deacons themselves agreed with their supervisors, but they made some distinctions. They thought a large minority of parishioners, priests, and lay staff with whom they worked did not adequately understand the identity of the deacon. But they did not think this was true of bishops and pastors.

In their write-in comments, more than a few deacons complained that they are too often thought by the laity and the parish staff to be either "incomplete priests" or "more advanced laity." A majority of their wives agreed with the statement, "I sometimes think most laity do not really understand that deacons are not 'priest-assistants' but ordained clergy in our church." One poignantly noted, "Deacons are not treated as clergy or as lay persons but as someone who is forever infringing on others' territories." On the other hand, lay leaders said they did not perceive any large problem regarding "deacon identity." The data suggest that they are simply less interested in the question than are deacons themselves and their supervisors. Parish leaders are mostly interested in the quality of the religious services available in their parish, and they are pleased and grateful that their deacons effectively contribute to them.

As the diaconate has unfolded in the first decades after its restoration, deacons have largely occupied parish places previously filled either entirely by priests or entirely by laity. The deacons' initial expectations, their formation and training programs, their internships, their actual work—all their primary diaconal influences and experiences—intertwine to draw them more narrowly into precisely those areas, roles, and behaviors already occupied by parish priests or staff. Except for the theologically sophisticated, it seems entirely natural that laity would view their deacons as either underqualified priests or overqualified laity. The vast majority of the lay leaders seem to base their ideas about the diaconate mostly on informal observation. They define the diaconate in terms of what they see deacons doing in their own parishes. Supervisors and lay leaders agree that there is little regular catechesis on the role of the permanent diaconate provided for parishioners.

Serving Beyond the Parish

While the deacons often mention service to others in their written comments, the category "to influence social change" rarely appeared. Few reported attempting or having any influence on local or national politics. Few reported much training in the areas of Catholic social thought, ministries, or direct human services.

To a question about social teaching, only 12 percent responded that it received "a very strong emphasis" in their studies and formation, and only an additional 20 percent were able to indicate at least "somewhat."

Lay leaders agreed. They said that they only very occasionally hear a deacon preach about social ministry or the social teaching of the Church. Likewise, deacons gave only mediocre ratings to their formation preparation when asked if they were prepared "to use social referral agencies like Catholic Charities and the Family Life Bureau." Less than one-third said this preparation was good or excellent; more than one-third said it was poor or even absent. Those few deacons working in non parish-based ministries report that their training was mostly "on-the-job" and subsequent to their formation program.

While the deacons tend to say they have at times preached on Catholic social teaching, very few were able to say they had even read the most prominent contemporary examples of this tradition. For example, the vast majority have not read the pastoral letters *The Challenge of Peace* and *Economic Justice for All* or the papal encyclicals *On Human Work* or *Centesimus Annus* ("On the 100th Anniversary"). Sixty percent are not familiar with the term "the consistent ethic of life." Only 13 percent of the lay leaders were able to say they "regularly" have heard their parish deacon preach on the Church's social teaching on justice and peace.[9]

The deacons' reading seems eclectic. Some said they read many books, some said none. The books they noted comprise a very diverse list—ranging from Thomas à Kempis to *The Velveteen Rabbit*. They seldom mentioned a work dealing with the theology of peace and justice. In fact, apart from topics of counseling in general and death and dying in particular, no "issue" book was mentioned.

Deacons Reflect on Their Future

We provided spaces on the questionnaire for visions of the future. In all of our samples most respondents anticipated diaconate futures pretty much like their experiences of the present ministries of deacons. The deacons' visions mostly involved better understanding, more acceptance, and clearer identities. Very few laity expressed a desire for anything more than what their deacons were already doing. The general direction of these remarks probably should be considered as understandably predictable.

Deacons themselves did not give as motivations for entering the diaconate an explicit desire to help the Church more effectively serve the community or to make her social teaching better known. Overwhelmingly, they said they were motivated by the opportunity for a mostly local ecclesial ministry of service that might deepen their own spiritual lives and give them a more powerful sense of purpose and place in life. These motivations are deeply shared by their spouses, implicitly accepted by their parishioners, and then explicitly encouraged by their supervisors, who are almost always pastors who find themselves increasingly dependent on deacons for the liturgical and sacramental ministries once done solely by priests. Their formation programs seem not to have challenged their initial parish-based vision of ecclesial service. Little in their postordination experiences seems likely to challenge it.[10]

The deacons reported an active spiritual life. In the course of a week, 76 percent read the Bible, 56 percent read spiritual authors, and 51 percent say the rosary. Forty-eight percent said the Divine Office "centers" or "plays a major role" in their spiritual life. Almost one-half said they receive the sacrament of penance at least every couple of months, and only 8 percent said "almost never."

Only one-half said they have a spiritual director, a decline from the two-thirds who had one in 1981. Their contacts with their pastor-supervisor are mainly task oriented. Besides, their pastor-supervisor's horizon is also parish bound. They are not likely to have received any specific training for supervising their deacons. Most said they either never read or do not recall the *1984 NCCB Guidelines for the Permanent Diaconate.* They are not likely to have read specific diaconate material or to have been in any close contact with either the diocesan or national deacons' office.[11] The norms for deacon accountability are mostly tacit and are unlikely to lead their supervisors and directors to encourage them into any less familiar or more adventuresome roles.

Very few parishes have written mission statements for their deacons.[12] The lay leaders reported that issues of accountability and role are largely determined through the single channel of the pastor. Although they seem prompted mostly by the generic good sense of the idea rather than any felt need to review priorities, the great majority of lay leaders support the idea of a written mission statement for deacons serving in their parish.

If it is desirable to move the ministry at least somewhat beyond its current overwhelming focus on parish life, our study shows that the impetus for this would need to come from the diocesan bishop, because the majority of deacons, their supervisors, and parish lay leaders assume that diaconal ministry is parish based. Otherwise their future ministries seem destined to tie them even more closely to parish life.

With very few exceptions, the deacons themselves find great satisfaction in their parish work, their pastor-supervisors find them increasingly indispensable, and parish leaders are content to have them as increasingly necessary adjuncts to their busy priests. Still, there are some indications from the data that even within this context of parish success and needs, some deacons would be open to appeals for service in less familiar and more innovative ministries. Significantly, almost all deacons said they are available for opportunities to learn of new needs in the Church and new challenges to her mission.[13] Only about one-third of the deacons said they *don't* attend more than a couple of seminars, lectures, or diocesan discussion groups each year. They also expressed a strong consensus that "field training should be more carefully chosen to better serve diocesan and community needs" (53% agree strongly and 29% somewhat). It is worth noting that the 1981 study found that about one-third favored "more emphasis on pastoral/field training in formation programs."

When asked, "What is your understanding of incardination?" deacons ranked first "being attached to a diocese" and second "being an extension of the bishop." When asked, "Do you understand your obligations and rights as a cleric in accordance with the provisions of the 1983 *Code of Canon Law*?" 79 percent responded "yes."

Since lay leaders have defined the role and mission of deacons mostly in terms of the *direct personal experience* of what they have seen deacons do, it is likely that laity will only reshape their conception of the diaconate and its meaning for the Church as deacons themselves deepen their conception of ministry.

Conclusions

We provided spaces on each questionnaire for visions of the future. In all our samples, most respondents anticipated that in the future, deacons will continue to function in the ways they function today. The deacons' visions mostly involved better understanding, more acceptance, and clearer identities. Very few laity expressed a desire for anything more than what their deacons were already doing. The general direction of these remarks probably should be considered as understandably predictable.

Deacons themselves did not give as motivations for entering the diaconate a desire to better help the Church, better serve the community, or to make her social teaching better known. Overwhelmingly, they said they were motivated by the opportunity for a mostly ecclesial ministry of service that might deepen their own spiritual life and give them a more powerful sense of purpose and place in life. These motivations are deeply shared by their spouses, are implicitly accepted by their parishioners, and then are explicitly encouraged by their supervisors, who are almost always pastors who find themselves increasingly dependent on them for the liturgical and sacramental ministries once done solely by priests. Their formation programs seem not to have challenged their initial parish-based vision of ecclesial service. Not much in their postordination experiences seems likely to challenge it. One-half said they have no spiritual director. Their contacts with their pastor-supervisor are mainly task oriented. Besides, their pastor-supervisor's horizon is also parish bound. They are not likely to have received any specific training for supervising their deacons. Most said they either have never read or do not recall the *1984 NCCB Guidelines for the Permanent Diaconate*. They are not likely to have read specific diaconate material or have been in any close contact with either the diocesan or national deacons' offices. The norms for deacon accountability are mostly tacit and are unlikely to lead their supervisors and directors to encourage them into less familiar or more adventuresome roles.

Very few parishes have written mission statements for their deacons. The lay leaders reported that issues of accountability and role are largely determined through the single channel of the pastor. Although they seem prompted mostly by the generic good sense of the idea rather than any felt need to review priorities, the great majority of lay leaders support the idea of a written ministerial agreement for deacons serving in their parish.

With very few exceptions, the deacons themselves find great satisfaction in their parish work, their pastor-supervisors find them increasingly indispensable, and parish leaders are content to have them as increasingly necessary adjuncts to their busy priests. Still, there are some modest indications from the data that even within this context of success and need, some deacons would be open to appeals for service in less familiar and more innovative ministries. Significantly, almost all deacons said that they are available for opportunities to learn of the new needs in the Church and new challenges to her mission. About one-third of the deacons say they don't attend more than a couple of seminars, lectures, or diocesan discussion groups each year. They also express a strong consensus that "field training should be more carefully chosen to better serve diocesan and community needs" (53% agree "strongly" and 29% "somewhat").

When asked, "What is your understanding of incardination?" deacons ranked first "being attached to a diocese" and second "being an extension of the bishop." When asked, "Do you understand your obligations and rights as a cleric in accordance with the provisions of the 1983 *Code of Canon Law?*" 79 percent responded "yes."

Since lay leaders have defined the role and mission of deacons mostly in terms of their *direct personal experience* of what they have seen deacons do, it is likely that laity will only reshape their conception of the diaconate and its meaning for the Church as deacons themselves deepen their conception of the ministry.

CONCLUSIONS DRAWN FROM THE DATA

1. CENTRAL FINDING: The restored Order of the Diaconate, largely parish based, has been successful and increasingly important for the life of the Church. The primary challenges of the diaconate for the future are to broaden its ministries beyond its largely successful and increasingly indispensable adaptation to parish life and to emphasize more strongly that deacons, through ordination, are called to be model, animator, and facilitator of ministries of charity and justice within the local church.

2. The enthusiastic acceptance of the diaconate by parish lay leaders is widespread. The majority foresaw a growth in the diaconate in the context of declining numbers of parish priests. Lay leaders rated the deacon's contribution to parish life very highly, most successful in traditional roles. Fifty-two percent of lay leaders rated deacons' preaching as about the same in quality as they would rate priests; 31 percent rated priests' homilies as higher in quality. Fifty-one percent of the lay leaders did not think that ordination was necessary for the ministries performed by deacons in their parishes.

3. The wives of deacons are supportive of their husband's ministry and consider their family greatly enriched by his ordination and service. As a result of being part of the diaconate, the deacons and their wives had more enriching experiences, met more people on deeper levels, and had more to share—all of which brought them human and spiritual growth.

4. Problems associated with the identity and acceptance of the deacon are reported in the larger context of high satisfaction. They are remediable by better communication and personal relations.

5. The median age of the deacons is 60. The majority are Caucasian, married, college educated, deeply spiritual, and highly motivated toward service. They believe that their ministry has enriched their relationship with their wives and children.

6. About one-fifth of the deacons have minority backgrounds with one-half of those describing themselves as "Hispanic-Latino." The obvious challenge is to recruit more deacons from minority communities.

7. Supervisors of deacons in ministry, most of whom are pastors where deacons serve, described their deacons as "able" in performing their duties. Eighty-eight percent of the supervisors rated their deacons as "very effective" to "somewhat effective" in pastoral care of the sick; 86 percent "very effective" to "somewhat effective" in preparing and giving homilies, and "effective" in sacramental service such as baptisms, marriages, and liturgies, but less so in promoting human and civil rights.

8. From the data—including written comments—we may conclude that the vast majority of supervisors and lay leaders regard their deacons as clearly necessary, judge them effective in their ministries, and find them satisfactorily trained. However, they are evenly divided over whether the deacons' ordination is important for the actual ministries they ably perform.

9. The most common prediction for the future was the neutral judgment that there will be fewer priests and more deacons who would increasingly function as "parish administrators," "parish-life coordinators," or "satellite-parish leaders." This scenario was considered by some, but not all, a pragmatic response to the priest shortage, distorting the meaning of both priesthood and diaconate.

10. The data suggest the need for a more effective catechesis on the diaconate—especially for the laity who are most accepting of the deacon but least sure of the role of the deacon apart from his sacramental ministry, the "priest-assistant." Parish leaders are most interested in the quality of the religious services available in their parish and are pleased and grateful that their deacons effectively contribute to them. Lay leaders did not perceive any large problem regarding the identity of the deacon.

11. The majority of parish leaders supported the idea of a written mission statement for deacons serving in their parish.

ISSUES FOR THE FUTURE

1. How are the issues of the deacon's identity and acceptance to be resolved in light of the tendency of many to use the deacon to address the present shortage of priests?

2. Is there a need for a more determined recruitment of men for the diaconate from minority and less affluent communities? If so, how is this to be addressed?

3. How can preordination spiritual formation and postordination continuing spiritual direction of deacons be better addressed?

4. How can diocesan deacon formation programs be strengthened to address better the principles of Catholic social justice teaching? How can candidates be better prepared to use service agencies such as Catholic Charities and Family Life Bureaus for referral and as a source of training?

5. What are the best means of response to the demonstrated need for a more focused effort on the national and diocesan levels to form and challenge deacons toward roles and ministries more clearly differentiated from the ministerial priesthood?

6. What will be required in developing curricula for deacon formation that will more clearly orient deacons toward embodying and preaching issues of justice, human rights, and peace?

7. In what ways can diocesan formation programs be strengthened in the following areas:

- Field training and internships that are extraparochial and diocesan oriented
- Orientation/preparation days for wives by wives of deacons to explore the role of the wife of a deacon and the impact of ordination on the deacon's family
- Spiritual direction for and by deacons
- More focused communication and accountability systems joining supervisors and deacons into wider networks of diocesan and Church-wide concerns
- Promoting further the need for a written mission statement and a specific role delineation for deacons
- Promoting opportunities in evangelization

The challenge of the next decades will be to make these developments more theologically rich and thus to expand the deacon's sense of ministry, evangelization, and service continually, even beyond the parish.

NOTES

1. In this summary, the detailed statistics available in the appendix that contains the four surveys are cited infrequently. Excessive detail would defeat the point of a summary essay. Still, the reader should be mindful that almost every one of the declarative sentences might have further nuances based on the concrete statistical data. For example, while only 1 percent of the deacons said they would *not* recommend the diaconate to someone considering it, 30 percent indicated that they would recommend it *with reservations*. That tells us something worth attending to. We should also explicitly acknowledge at the outset that the advantages and disadvantages of a national sample are necessarily intertwined. Since a national sample generalizes from numerous and sometimes contrary (or at least varied) local experiences and tendencies, the aggregate

tendencies—the big picture—it reports might not altogether fit any real diocese, parish, deacon, or deacon's family. But in the Roman Catholic tradition, each diocese, each parish, each deacon, and each deacon's family is taught and encouraged to consider as part of its own more specific and immediate realities the larger—and thus more general—question, "How is the order of the deacons serving the Church universal?" Big pictures blur some important details; but they can, at least a bit, serve to focus the aspirations of each of their parts. The reader should note the appendix where other studies and other reports are cited for further reading and reflection.

2. Eugene F. Hemrick and Joseph Shields, *A National Summary of the Permanent Diaconate In the United States* (Washington, D.C.: United States Catholic Conference, 1981).

3. For a discussion of the process of sampling and its reliability, see Appendix B.

4. The *1994 Annual Statistical Report on the Permanent Diaconate in the United States*, issued by the Secretariat for the Diaconate, reports that 57 dioceses have a formal policy for retirement and that their mandatory age for deacons to retire ranges from 70 to 75 (the mode).

5. On the question of deacon and spousal satisfaction, the 1981 study offered a comment that continues to apply to our findings: "One must not overlook a certain psycho-spiritual phenomenon that comes with the stages of life. In middle age, having pursued a career and raised a family, one not uncommonly turns one's thoughts to the deeper meaning of existence. Spiritual realities take on a greater significance. In the permanent diaconate, an environment and support system are afforded whereby a man, his wife, and family can respond to this grace. From the study's data reflecting a high degree of diaconal fulfillment, it would seem just such a psycho-spiritual phenomenon is occurring."

6. The Vatican's yearbook reported that at the end of 1993, 349 of the world's parishes were entrusted to deacons, 131 to religious brothers, 1,068 to religious women, and 1,614 to lay people. The yearbook reports a total of 404,560 diocesan and religious order priests worldwide, a decline of seventy-six from 1992. The yearbook reports a worldwide Catholic population of about 965 million, an increase of about 6.3 million over 1992.

7. The 1981 survey reported that among the deacons "only 5.3 percent envisioned the diaconate as a stepping-stone to a married clergy or as a movement leading to women priests."

8. The *1994 Annual Statistical Report on the Permanent Diaconate in the United States* reports that sixty deacons are serving as full-time administrators of parishes and forty are serving part-time. About 10 percent of the deacons receive some salary for their ministry: 887 are salaried as deacon in full-time ministry, 236 in part-time ministry; 524 are salaried in positions such as diocesan director of finance, director of the diocesan diaconate program, and director of religious education.

9. When the 1981 study asked deacons about changes in their training, none mentioned courses about the social teachings of the Church. The study states: "When asked *'As a result of your lived experience, what aspects of your formation program need to be improved or changed?'* 35 percent of the deacons said there should be more emphasis on pastoral/field training, 20 percent favored more emphasis on dogmatic and moral theology, 16 percent said ascetical theology and prayer should be given first priority, 4 percent asked for more continuing education after ordination, 3 percent called for better screening of candidates, and 14 percent said nothing should be changed." While almost all the deacons in our sample said they have used Catholic social teachings in a sermon or have included them in their teaching, they also acknowledged that, for the most part, they have never read them "in their entirety." Usually far less than one-third (respectively, 30%; 37%; 10%; 12%; 22%; 16%) said

they had even read at least "a good part of" the Bishops' pastoral letters *The Challenge of Peace* and *Economic Justice for All* and the most recent Papal encyclicals *On Social Concern, On Human Work,* and *On the 100th Anniversary.*

10. The *1994 Statistical Report* shows that the vast majority of deacons ministered in parish settings (75%) or pastoral care of the sick (23%). Six percent reported family ministries and 7 percent youth ministries. For the following ministries the percentage participating never exceeded 5 percent: prison, substance abuse, homeless, hunger, AIDS, migrants/refugees, mental illness, abused and battered wives, disabled, racial and ethnic discrimination, and rural. It might be noted, however, that 5 percent, the percentage engaged in prison ministry, represents 573 deacons.

11. A newsletter or other means of written communication is published regularly in seventy-two dioceses.

12. The *1994 Statistical Report* says that fifty-six dioceses have a job description for deacons. In ninety-five dioceses, deacons sign a contract or agreement. The 1981 study found that about one-half had no job description.

13. Ninety-three dioceses have some form of deacons' organization or structure, ranging from formal councils to regular assemblies. Sixty-two relate directly to the bishop while forty-eight make appointments or recommendations for deacon participation in diocesan committees. Forty dioceses are members of the National Association of Deacon Organizations.

APPENDIX A

....

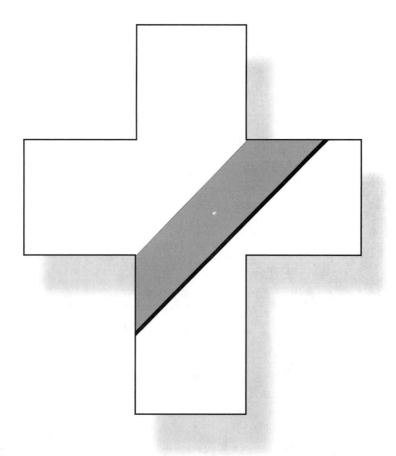

TABLE 1
GROWTH OF DIACONATE
1976-1993

Year	Growth (%)
1976	5.0
77	4.2
78	6.1
79	5.9
80	5.5
81	5.0
82	5.3
83	5.4
84	4.8
85	4.4
86	4.9
87	6.0
88	6.0
89	4.1
90	4.1
91	4.0
92	5.9
93	4.5

FIGURE 1
AGE GROUPINGS OF DEACONS

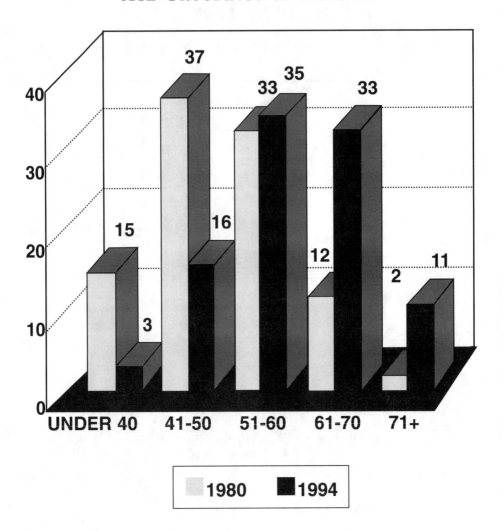

FIGURE 2
DEACONS IN THE U.S.A.

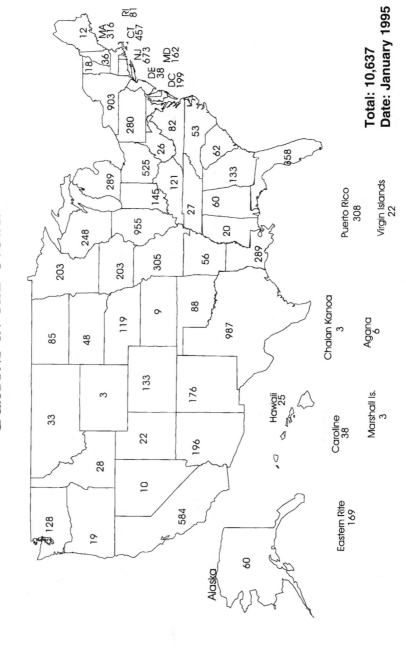

Alaska 60

Hawaii 25

Eastern Rite 169

Caroline 38

Marshall Is. 3

Chalan Kanoa 3

Agana 6

Puerto Rico 308

Virgin Islands 22

Total: 10,637
Date: January 1995

TABLE 2
DEACONS' TEAM SATISFACTION
WITH CO-MINISTERS

	Parish	Pastor	Deacons	Parish	Priest	Bishop Staff	Parish Council	Super-visor	Diocesan Office	Sisters
Feel like a team	90%	81%	77%	75%	75%	74%	67%	59%	56%	53%
Little to no feeling	8	17	9	14	22	23	16	8	22	10
Doesn't pertain	2	2	14	8	3	3	17	33	21	37

TABLE 3
VISION OF DEACONS' ROLE
BY FAMILY AND CO-MINISTERS

Vision	Wife	Children	Deacons	Bishop	Pastor	Parish Staff	Priests	Super- visor	Parish Council	Parish	Sisters
Clear/somewhat clear	93%	83%	82%	79%	74%	67%	60%	59%	56%	56%	48%
Some/much confusion	3	8	16	12	13	24	38	6	24	41	13
Don't know	0	2	2	8	2	3	2	3	7	2	5
Not Applicable	4	7	1	1	1	5	0	32	13	1	33

TABLE 4
DIACONAL MINISTRIES
RATED BY SUPERVISORS

	Very/somewhat effective	Ineffective	Deacon doesn't perform ministry	Don't know
Sacramental activities	94.8%	2.1%	2.1%	1.0%
Visit sick/elderly	88.5	2.3	7.8	1.3
Homilies	86.1	6.2	6.7	1.0
Religious Ed.	79.9	3.7	13.6	2.9
Work with poor	71.5	3.9	18.6	6.0
Administration	70.0	6.0	31.2	2.9
RCIA	69.4	3.7	24.0	2.9
Social Justice Teaching	67.5	8.2	18.1	6.1
Evangelization	66.7	5.3	22.1	5.9
Counseling	61.6	5.6	24.9	7.9
Leader of prayer groups	58.3	4.5	33.5	3.4
Pro-Life	57.7	4.3	30.1	8.0
Promote civil rights	52.9	7.0	30.6	9.4
Work with small base communities	36.4	5.8	50.0	7.5
Prison ministry	32.6	4.3	52.8	9.8

APPENDIX B

....

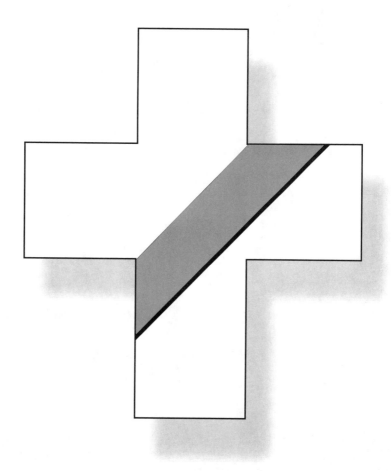

SAMPLING

The total number of returns to Phase I, The Study of Permanent Deacons, is 5,369 out of 9,000, or a 60 percent return. The total number of returns to Phase II, The Study of Deacons' Wives, is 1,194 out of 1,850, or a 64 percent return.

In the case of Phase I, it would be impractical to process all 5,369 returns. A good random sample gives the same results, therefore 3,073 questionnaires were randomly picked out of the total number received. Figure 3 gives an overall picture of the number of questionnaires sampled from any one diocese. The margin of error in a sample of this size is no more than three +/– percentage points.

It should be noted in Figure 3 that dioceses that reflect no deacons being selected do so either because they do not have the permanent diaconate (there are twenty-seven such dioceses) or because they did not send in the names of their deacons as requested for this study. Also, a diocese may not be represented because it has few deacons and the sampling missed them. Or it could be that the deacon removed the name of the diocese on the return questionnaire, making the diocese anonymous.

To ensure that African Americans, Hispanics, Asians, Native Americans, Eskimos, and Aleuts were represented, any deacon in the 5,369 returns found to be of these cultures was included. Hence, within the random sample, there is a selected sample of cultures other than white Anglos.

WHAT IS RANDOM SAMPLING
AND WHY IS IT RELIABLE?

When large populations like the U.S. census are surveyed, the mass of data that are returned makes it impossible to process every single person. Thanks to the reliable laws of probability, researchers can take a random sample of the population, analyze it, and usually be 95 percent to 100 percent confident that the sample reliably represents the entire population.

When a sample is called "random," it describes not the data in the sample, but the process by which the sample was obtained. A sample of size n is said to be a random sample if it was obtained by a process that gave each possible combination of n items in the population the same chance of being the sample actually drawn.

The reasons for sampling are many. It is based on certain fixed laws of probability that ensure reliability. It avoids unnecessary cost and time, and it lowers the possibilities for error. Avoiding added cost, time, and error, however, are not the main reasons for choosing random sampling over total sampling. Rather, the law of big numbers makes random sampling desirable and reliable. It is based on the laws of probability that state the larger the sample, the less variablility there will be be in the sample proportion. The probability that p will be within a given range of P is greater for samples of 100 than for samples of 20 from the same population, and still greater for samples of 1,000. In the case of the permanent diaconate study, the samples were large enough to reduce the margin of error to a few percentage points.

Phase II and Phase III also used random sampling. In Phase II, The Study of Deacons' Wives, 1,850 names and addresses of wives were randomly taken from the 5,369 deacon questionnaires. These 1,850 names constituted the random sample. Of the 1,850 questionnaires sent out, 1,194 (64%) were returned.

In Phase III, A Study of Supervisors of Deacons, 1,719 names and addresses of supervisors were picked out of the 5,369 deacon questionnaires; 533 (31%) were returned and processed.

In Phase IV, A Study of Parish Councils, 1,685 names and addresses were picked out of 7,000 deacon questionnaires; 581 (34%) were returned and processed.

The large samples that were drawn for the three phases of the diaconate study and the equally large returns are reason to say that the study on the diaconate reliably represents its status in the United States.

SURVEY RESULTS

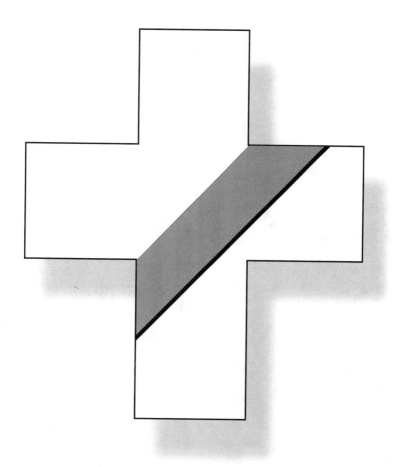

National Conference of Catholic Bishops
Diaconate Study
for Parish Council Members

1. How many years have you been on the parish council? . . 5.4 Mean

2. What is your parish council title?

3. How many permanent deacons presently serve
   your parish? . . . . 1.8 Mean

4. In 1968 the permanent diaconate was restored in the United States.
From what you have observed of all permanent deacons who have
served in the parish, what is your general reaction to the restoration of
the diaconate?
   1. Very positive 59.1
   2. Positive 34.5
   3. Neutral 5.2
   4. Negative 0.9
   5. Very negative 0.2
   6. I really don't know 0.2

5. How would you rate your understanding of the role of the permanent diaconate?
   1. Very good understanding 29.3
   2. A good understanding 46.7
   3. A fair understanding 20.9
   4. Very little understanding 2.8
   5. No understanding to speak of 0.3

6. What has best helped you understand the role of the permanent
deacon? (Write none, if nothing helped.)

Using the scale below, how much do you agree with the following?

7. The diocesan bishop in general is enthusiastic about the permanent diaconate.
   1. Strongly agree 24.9
   2. Agree 38.3
   3. Disagree 4.2
   4. Strongly disagree 1.9
   5. I don't know 30.7

8. The parish priests are enthusiastic about the permanent diaconate.
   1. Strongly agree 34.9
   2. Agree 45.8
   3. Disagree 9.2
   4. Strongly disagree 1.6
   5. I don't know 8.6

9. Parishioners understand the role of deacons for the most part.
   1. Strongly agree 4.5
   2. Agree 62.4
   3. Disagree 22.4
   4. Strongly disagree 4.3
   5. I don't know 6.3

10. In terms of my own experience, I think priests have grown even more supportive of the diaconate than they were over the last ten years.
   1. Strongly agree 27.2
   2. Agree 47.3
   3. Disagree 8.0
   4. Strongly disagree 0.9
   5. I don't know 16.6

11. I believe parishioners have come to understand the role of deacon much better over the last ten years.
   1. Strongly agree 19.0
   2. Agree 57.0
   3. Disagree 13.6
   4. Strongly disagree 2.1
   5. I don't know 8.3

12. I now think the permanent diaconate is even more needed than when it was first restored.
    1. Strongly agree 67.1
    2. Agree. 25.4
    3. Disagree 3.3
    4. Strongly disagree 1.2
    5. I don't know 0.9

13. I expect the diaconate will grow substantially in numbers in the next five years in our parish.
    1. Strongly agree 18.9
    2. Agree 22.1
    3. Disagree 26.5
    4. Strongly disagree 5.7
    5. I don't know 26.8

14. Overall, how well is the deacon introduced to the community he serves?
    1. Very well 51.2
    2. Somewhat well 36.4
    3. Not well 10.0
    4. Almost never happens 2.0
    5. It is almost or totally nonexistent 0.5

Using the scale below, how much ongoing instruction on the permanent diaconate is happening with the following groups?
15. Parishioners in general
    1. It is happening on a very regular basis. 5.9
    2. It is happening on a somewhat regular basis. 16.4
    3. It is somewhat irregular. 21.6
    4. It is very irregular. 19.2
    5. It is almost to totally nonexistent. 33.2
    6. I really don't know. 3.7

16. The parish council
    1. It is happening on a very regular basis. 10.3
    2. It is happening on a somewhat regular basis. 22.5
    3. It is somewhat irregular. 21.5
    4. It is very irregular. 15.6
    5. It is almost to totally nonexistent. 28.5
    6. I really don't know. 1.6

17. Parish organizations
    1. It is happening on a very regular basis. 5.6
    2. It is happening on a somewhat regular basis. 18.3
    3. It is somewhat irregular. 21.4
    4. It is very irregular. 15.1
    5. It is almost to totally nonexistent. 29.9
    6. I really don't know. 9.7

18. Parish priest(s)
    1. It is happening on a very regular basis. 19.8
    2. It is happening on a somewhat regular basis. 15.5
    3. It is somewhat irregular. 8.0
    4. It is very irregular. 3.5
    5. It is almost to totally nonexistent. 7.8
    6. I really don't know. 45.4

19. Do deacons in your parish have a written mission statement?
    1. Yes 19.3
    2. No 15.3
    3. I don't know 65.3

20. Do you think deacons need a written mission statement?
    1. Yes 77.4
    2. No 22.6

21. If yes, why do you think they need it?

22. In general, how would you describe the relationship between a deacon's wife and the priests with whom he ministers?
   1. Very warm and respectful 49.0
   2. Somewhat warm and respectful 21.0
   3. Somewhat distant 5.6
   4. Very distant 2.1
   5. I really can't say 22.2

23. In general, how much collaboration do you see between deacons and their pastors?
   1. Very much collaboration 53.7
   2. Some collaboration 33.7
   3. Very little collaboration 8.5
   4. No collaboration 0.9
   5. I don't know 3.9

24. In general, do the deacons you know express satisfaction or dissatisfaction over this degree of collaboration?
   1. Satisfaction 58.4
   2. Dissatisfaction 13.7
   3. I don't know 27.9

25. In general, how much collaboration do you see between deacons and paid parish staff?
   1. Very much collaboration 35.9
   2. Some collaboration 40.2
   3. Very little collaboration 8.4
   4. No collaboration 2.3
   5. I don't know 13.2

26. In general, how much do you see deacons and priests collaborating as a team?
   1. To a great degree 43.2
   2. To a fair degree 42.6
   3. Very little 12.3
   4. To almost no degree 1.9

27. How often does the council meet with the parish deacon(s) to discuss the deacon's ministry?
    1. It is done very regularly. 8.8
    2. It is done somewhat regularly. 8.3
    3. It is done irregularly. 12.7
    4. It is seldom done. 19.2
    5. It is never done. 47.3
    6. I don't know. 3.7

28. In what ministries have you met or worked with deacons?

29. Using the scale below, please tell us how effective (overall) you found the deacons in the ministries you specified above.

                1 2 3 4 5 6 7 8 9
                Not Effective   Very Effective
. . . . 7.2 Mean

30. How frequently do(es) the deacon(s) preach at Mass?
    1. Very frequently 24.5
    2. Somewhat frequently 47.3
    3. Seldom 18.6
    4. Never 9.6

31. Compared to homilies preached generally by priests, would you say that in quality those preached generally by the deacon(s) are:
    1. Much higher in quality 5.7
    2. A little higher in quality 11.0
    3. About the same in quality 52.4
    4. A little lower in quality 22.8
    5. Much lower in quality 8.2

32. Compared to homilies generally preached by priests, would you say that in content those preached generally by the deacon(s) contain:
    1. Much more content 6.9
    2. A little more content 13.4
    3. About the same content 56.7
    4. A little lower in content 18.5
    5. Much lower in content 4.6

33. Are there any expectations of deacons that you have that are not being met?
    1. Yes 22.6
    2. No 77.4

34. If yes, please specify them.

35. Since your parish has had a deacon(s), has there also been any increase in numbers and quality of parishioner participation in your parish?
    1. Yes 48.6
    2. No 51.4

36. If yes, please tell us if (and how) the deacon(s) have contributed to this increase.

37. Have you personally been affected by the ministries of the deacon(s)?
    1. Yes 62.2
    2. No 37.8

38. If yes, in what way?

39. Could the ministries that deacon(s) perform be performed equally by a lay person or this same person without ordination?
    1. No, definitely not 22.4
    2. No, probably not 28.9
    3. Maybe 22.2
    4. Yes, probably 17.7
    5. Yes, definitely could be done by a lay person 8.8

Using the following scale, how much has the ministry of the deacon(s) in your parish contributed to the work of:

40. Pastor
1. Much 53.1
2. Somewhat 30.9
3. Not much 6.0
4. None 2.1
5. I don't know 7.9

41. Parish priests
1. Much 44.2
2. Somewhat 34.4
3. Not much 7.1
4. None 4.4
5. I don't know 9.8

42. Lay staff
1. Much 24.5
2. Somewhat 38.7
3. Not much 16.2
4. None 5.2
5. I don't know 15.3

43. Lay ministers
1. Much 30.6
2. Somewhat 40.4
3. Not much 14.4
4. None 5.0
5. I don't know 9.5

44. Laity
1. Much 26.7
2. Somewhat 44.0
3. Not much 12.9
4. None 5.0
5. I don't know 11.4

Using the scale below, how much do you agree with the following statements?

45. Deacons play an important role in getting the lay people in my church more actively involved in community activities.
    1. Strongly agree 27.3
    2. Agree somewhat 40.9
    3. Somewhat disagree 16.7
    4. Strongly disagree 9.9
    5. I don't know 5.2

46. In our parish, it seems that most of the parishioners who are regular mass attenders do not adequately understand the difference between a deacon and priest.
    1. Strongly agree 5.2
    2. Agree somewhat 19.7
    3. Somewhat disagree 22.5
    4. Strongly disagree 49.6
    5. I don't know 3.0

Using the scale below, how would you rate the deacon(s) on the following?

47. In our parish, the deacon preaches on the Church's social teaching regarding justice and peace.
    1. Regularly 13.7
    2. Sometimes 27.3
    3. Occasionally 21.5
    4. Rarely 18.4
    5. I can't say 6.0
    6. Deacon(s) doesn't preach 13.1

48. Does your parish council have guidelines about how frequently supervisors and deacons should meet with them?
    1. Yes 12.0
    2. No 78.0
    3. I don't know 10.0

49. What are the three most common concerns the parish council discusses with the deacon(s)?

Although a parish may have more or less than three deacons, please think of the deacons that are in your parish and answer the following for the first three that come to mind.

Do you believe that the deacon(s) in your parish would devote the same time to his/their present ministry if not ordained? Put the number that corresponds to your response on the blank.

50. Deacon-1
1. No, definitely would not without ordination 16.6
2. No, probably not 28.2
3. Maybe, would not, maybe would 17.5
4. Yes, probably 25.7
5. Yes, definitely would be as willing without ordination 11.9

51. Deacon-2
1. No, definitely would not without ordination 12.0
2. No, probably not 32.9
3. Maybe, would not, maybe would 19.4
4. Yes, probably 27.2
5. Yes, definitely would be as willing without ordination 8.5

52. Deacon-3
1. No, definitely would not without ordination 12.7
2. No, probably not 24.6
3. Maybe, would not, maybe would 21.4
4. Yes, probably 27.0
5. Yes, definitely would be as willing without ordination 14.3

Did you know the deacon(s) in your parish before he/they became a candidate for the permanent diaconate?

53. D-1
1. Yes 47.9
2. No 52.1

54. D-2
1. Yes 45.1
2. No 54.9

55. **D-3**
    1. Yes 53.1
    2. No 46.9

*If yes, did the parish council encourage this man/men to pursue
ordination?*
56. **D-1**
    1. Yes 29.5
    2. No 70.5

57. **D-2**
    1. Yes 25.8
    2. No 74.2

58. **D-3**
    1. Yes 27.9
    2. No 72.1

*If it had been in your power, would you have agreed to the ordination
of the man/men to the diaconate?*
59. **D-1**
    1. Yes 94.3
    2. No 5.7

60. **D-2**
    1. Yes 91.7
    2. No 8.3

61. **D-3**
    1. Yes 87.3
    2. No 12.7

Using the scale below, how would you rate the effectiveness of deacons in the following?

LITURGICAL CELEBRATION

62. D-1
1. Very effective 61.1
2. Somewhat effective 31.9
3. Ineffective 5.2
4. Deacon does not perform this ministry 1.0
5. I really don't know 0.3
6. Doesn't pertain 0.3

63. D-2
1. Very effective 46.4
2. Somewhat effective 40.8
3. Ineffective 7.3
4. Deacon does not perform this ministry 3.1
5. I really don't know 1.7
6. Doesn't pertain 0.7

64. D-3
1. Very effective 37.6
2. Somewhat effective 43.2
3. Ineffective 13.6
4. Deacon does not perform this ministry 1.6
5. I really don't know 3.2
6. Doesn't pertain 0.8

RELIGIOUS EDUCATION

65. D-1
1. Very effective 43.4
2. Somewhat effective 28.5
3. Ineffective 4.5
4. Deacon does not perform this ministry 11.3
5. I really don't know 9.1
6. Doesn't pertain 3.1

66. D-2

1. Very effective 33.7
2. Somewhat effective 27.1
3. Ineffective 6.6
4. Deacon does not perform this ministry 17.0
5. I really don't know 11.8
6. Doesn't pertain 3.8

67. D-3

1. Very effective 25.6
2. Somewhat effective 28.8
3. Ineffective 7.2
4. Deacon does not perform this ministry 16.0
5. I really don't know 15.2
6. Doesn't pertain 7.2

Participation in parish/diocesan administration

68. D-1

1. Very effective 33.0
2. Somewhat effective 25.2
3. Ineffective 7.5
4. Deacon does not perform this ministry 16.3
5. I really don't know 14.5
6. Doesn't pertain 3.5

69. D-2

1. Very effective 16.8
2. Somewhat effective 27.0
3. Ineffective 7.4
4. Deacon does not perform this ministry 24.9
5. I really don't know 18.9
6. Doesn't pertain 4.9

70. D-3

1. Very effective 16.3
2. Somewhat effective 16.3
3. Ineffective 07.3
4. Deacon does not perform this ministry 25.2
5. I really don't know 25.2
6. Doesn't pertain 9.8

WORK WITH THE POOR
71. D-1
1. Very effective 29.2
2. Somewhat effective 22.9
3. Ineffective 2.8
4. Deacon does not perform this ministry 13.6
5. I really don't know 29.8
6. Doesn't pertain 1.8

72. D-2
1. Very effective 22.3
2. Somewhat effective 21.2
3. Ineffective 4.9
4. Deacon does not perform this ministry 13.4
5. I really don't know 36.0
6. Doesn't pertain 2.1

73. D-3
l. Very effective 23.8
2. Somewhat effective 19.8
3. Ineffective 4.0
4. Deacon does not perform this ministry 11.9
5. I really don't know 34.1
6. Doesn't pertain 6.3

PRO-LIFE MOVEMENT
74. D-1
1. Very effective 25.2
2. Somewhat effective 25.0
3. Ineffective 2.1
4. Deacon does not perform this ministry 13.2
5. I really don't know 32.2
6. Doesn't pertain 2.3

75. D-2
1. Very effective 21.2
2. Somewhat effective 21.2
3. Ineffective 3.2
4. Deacon does not perform this ministry 14.5
5. I really don't know 37.8
6. Doesn't pertain 2.1

76. D-3
1. Very effective 24.2
2. Somewhat effective 17.7
3. Ineffective 3.2
4. Deacon does not perform this ministry 16.1
5. I really don't know 34.7
6. Doesn't pertain 4.0

PRISON MINISTRY
77. D-1
1. Very effective 11.2
2. Somewhat effective 6.7
3. Ineffective 2.1
4. Deacon does not perform this ministry 27.9
5. I really don't know 36.2
6. Doesn't pertain 15.8

78. D-2
1. Very effective 7.2
2. Somewhat effective 6.1
3. Ineffective 2.5
4. Deacon does not perform this ministry 33.3
5. I really don't know 38.4
6. Doesn't pertain 12.5

79. D-3
1. Very effective 9.9
2. Somewhat effective 3.3
3. Ineffective 3.3
4. Deacon does not perform this ministry 28.9
5. I really don't know 38.8
6. Doesn't pertain 15.7

WORK WITH SMALL BASE COMMUNITIES
80. D-1
1. Very effective 22.5
2. Somewhat effective 19.8
3. Ineffective 2.1
4. Deacon does not perform this ministry 14.5
5. I really don't know 33.0
6. Doesn't pertain 8.0

81. D-2
1. Very effective 18.6
2. Somewhat effective 19.4
3. Ineffective 2.5
4. Deacon does not perform this ministry 16.5
5. I really don't know 35.5
6. Doesn't pertain 7.5

82. D-3
1. Very effective 21.1
2. Somewhat effective 16.3
3. Ineffective 4.1
4. Deacon does not perform this ministry 17.9
5. I really don't know 33.3
6. Doesn't pertain 7.3

VISITING SICK/ELDERLY
83. D-1
1. Very effective 50.2
2. Somewhat effective 21.7
3. Ineffective 2.4
4. Deacon does not perform this ministry 5.1
5. I really don't know 19.8
6. Doesn't pertain 0.9

84. **D-2**
1. Very effective 36.5
2. Somewhat effective 25.3
3. Ineffective 2.1
4. Deacon does not perform this ministry 9.7
5. I really don't know 25.0
6. Doesn't pertain 1.4

85. **D-3**
1. Very effective 39.1
2. Somewhat effective 25.0
3. Ineffective 1.6
4. Deacon does not perform this ministry 5.5
5. I really don't know 25.0
6. Doesn't pertain 3.9

PROMOTING HUMAN AND CIVIL RIGHTS
86. **D-1**
1. Very effective 29.0
2. Somewhat effective 24.3
3. Ineffective 3.7
4. Deacon does not perform this ministry 12.0
5. I really don't know 28.2
6. Doesn't pertain 2.8

87. **D-2**
1. Very effective 22.3
2. Somewhat effective 27.0
3. Ineffective 2.8
4. Deacon does not perform this ministry 12.4
5. I really don't know 34.4
6. Doesn't pertain 1.1

88. **D-3**
1. Very effective 16.8
2. Somewhat effective 30.4
3. Ineffective 4.0
4. Deacon does not perform this ministry 12.0
5. I really don't know 32.8
6. Doesn't pertain 4.0

SACRAMENTAL ACTIVITIES E.G., BAPTISMS, MARRIAGES
89. D-1
1. Very effective 63.5
2. Somewhat effective 21.6
3. Ineffective 2.3
4. Deacon does not perform this ministry 4.7
5. I really don't know 7.5
6. Doesn't pertain 0.5

90. D-2
1. Very effective 54.3
2. Somewhat effective 23.5
3. Ineffective 1.7
4. Deacon does not perform this ministry 7.3
5. I really don't know 12.8
6. Doesn't pertain 0.3

91. D-3
1. Very effective 48.8
2. Somewhat effective 25.2
3. Ineffective 0
4. Deacon does not perform this ministry 7.1
5. I really don't know 16.5
6. Doesn't pertain 2.4

MARRIAGE PREPARATION
92. D-1
1. Very effective 38.2
2. Somewhat effective 17.0
3. Ineffective 1.9
4. Deacon does not perform this ministry 15.4
5. I really don't know 24.9
6. Doesn't pertain 2.6

93. **D-2**
   1. Very effective 30.4
   2. Somewhat effective 18.5
   3. Ineffective 1.7
   4. Deacon does not perform this ministry 18.5
   5. I really don't know 27.6
   6. Doesn't pertain 3.1

94. **D-3**
   1. Very effective 26.4
   2. Somewhat effective 20.8
   3. Ineffective 1.6
   4. Deacon does not perform this ministry 16.0
   5. I really don't know 28.8
   6. Doesn't pertain 6.4

COUNSELING
95. **D-1**
   1. Very effective 27.7
   2. Somewhat effective 18.1
   3. Ineffective 2.5
   4. Deacon does not perform this ministry 11.6
   5. I really don't know 37.0
   6. Doesn't pertain 3.2

96. **D-2**
   1. Very effective 20.4
   2. Somewhat effective 19.7
   3. Ineffective 2.5
   4. Deacon does not perform this ministry 9.5
   5. I really don't know 44.7
   6. Doesn't pertain 3.2

97. **D-3**
   1. Very effective 18.5
   2. Somewhat effective 20.2
   3. Ineffective 4.8
   4. Deacon does not perform this ministry 8.1
   5. I really don't know 44.4
   6. Doesn't pertain 4.0

Rite of Christian Initiation of Adults (RCIA), Inquiry Classes
98. D-1
1. Very effective 41.9
2. Somewhat effective 16.1
3. Ineffective 2.8
4. Deacon does not perform this ministry 16.4
5. I really don't know 19.4
6. Doesn't pertain 3.4

99. D-2
1. Very effective 26.8
2. Somewhat effective 18.9
3. Ineffective 3.9
4. Deacon does not perform this ministry 22.9
5. I really don't know 22.1
6. Doesn't pertain 5.4

100. D-3
1. Very effective 26.2
2. Somewhat effective 18.9
3. Ineffective 4.1
4. Deacon does not perform this ministry 21.3
5. I really don't know 23.0
6. Doesn't pertain 6.6

Leader of Prayer Groups, Charismatics, Marriage Encounter
101. D-1
1. Very effective 31.7
2. Somewhat effective 20.6
3. Ineffective 3.5
4. Deacon does not perform this ministry 16.5
5. I really don't know 23.9
6. Doesn't pertain 3.7

102. **D-2**
   1. Very effective 24.0
   2. Somewhat effective 23.3
   3. Ineffective 3.1
   4. Deacon does not perform this ministry 17.1
   5. I really don't know 28.9
   6. Doesn't pertain 3.5

103. **D-3**
   1. Very effective 25.0
   2. Somewhat effective 21.0
   3. Ineffective 3.2
   4. Deacon does not perform this ministry 15.3
   5. I really don't know 29.0
   6. Doesn't pertain 6.5

104. Since its implementation in your parish, do you feel the ministry of the deacons turned out as you expected?
   1. Very much so 28.9
   2. Pretty much so 42.1
   3. I don't know 9.1
   4. Not quite 9.8
   5. Much different 4.4
   6. I can't say 5.6

105. If you answered, "not quite" or "much different" please tell us in what way(s).

106. As far as you know, does the formation of the deacon in your parish seem to be:
   1. Very adequate 48.3
   2. Somewhat adequate 33.4
   3. Somewhat inadequate 6.4
   4. Very inadequate 4.7
   5. I really don't know 7.1

107. If no, please list the three most evident areas of deficiency.

108. How effective do you believe the parish council's collaboration with parish deacons has been?
1. Very effective 18.8
2. Somewhat effective 31.6
3. Not very effective 21.6
4. Ineffective 23.0
5. I don't know 4.9

109. If you answered "not very" or "almost ineffective," please tell us why.

110. How well do you feel deacons are appropriately trained to work with women on the staff and in other leadership groups in the parish?
1. Very well 28.6
2. Fairly well 36.1
3. Somewhat poorly 5.3
4. Very poorly 3.5
5. I really don't know. 26.5

111. How well do you feel deacons are appropriately trained to work with women religious on the staff and in other leadership groups in the parish?
1. Very well 26.1
2. Fairly well 32.4
3. Somewhat poorly 5.7
4. Very poorly 2.1
5. I really don't know 33.6

112. What do you believe are the two most satisfying experiences deacons have?

113. What do you feel are the two most frustrating experiences deacons have?

114. What direction do you see the permanent diaconate taking in the next decade?

115. What direction would you like to see it taking?

116. In terms of the direction you indicated in the preceding question, what are the major obstacles you see to the permanent diaconate in the next decade?

117. Deacons sometimes speak of an "identity problem." Is this generally true in your experience?
    1. Yes 32.8
    2. No 67.2

118. If "yes," what are the major reasons for this?

119. In your experience, have the deacons' ministerial duties ever conflicted with their family obligations?
    1. Does not apply 8.8
    2. Often 7.8
    3. Sometimes 41.9
    4. Rarely 30.5
    5. Never 11.0

120. What is your age as of your last birthday? . . . . 52.3 Mean

121. What is your vocational status?
    1. Lay person 93.7
    2. Religious brother 0.3
    3. Religious sister 0.3
    4. Permanent deacon 1.9
    5. Priest 3.7

122. What is your gender?
    1. Female 33.2
    2. Male 66.8

123. How would you describe the work which occupies the largest portion of your weekly schedule?

124. If you work within a parish structure, which of the following best describes your position?
1. Does not pertain 55.1
2. Pastor 4.5
3. Associate pastor 0.4
4. Parish staff member 6.6
5. Other (describe) 33.5

125. If you are a priest, permanent deacon or member of a religious community, for how many years have you been ordained or professed? . . . . 19.3 Mean

126. What is the highest academic degree you have achieved?
1. Some high school 0.5
2. High school graduate 10.9
3. Some college 19.5
4. College degree 35.7
5. Master's degree or equivalent 29.8
6. Doctorate 3.6

127. What is your predominant racial/ethnic background?
1. African American 1.7
2. Caucasian 92.1
3. Hispanic 3.3
4. Native American 1.6
5. Asian 0.2
6. Other (describe) 1.0

128. Is there any question you think should have been asked about deacons that wasn't?

A National Study of the Permanent Diaconate Conducted by The NCCB Committee for the Permanent Diaconate

[1] In addition to a personal call from God, what primarily caused you to consider the diaconate?
1. I was inspired by the ministry of another deacon......... 10.7
2. I was inspired by the ministry of a priest. 10.7
3. I felt a need to deepen the service(s) I was already giving to the Church. 61.0
4. My wife and family encouraged me to become a deacon. ... 4.6
5. Other. 13.0

[2] If you answered #3, what service(s) were you giving to the Church?

[3] Did you ever consider studying for the priesthood?
1. Yes 52.4
2. No 47.6

[4] If yes, how much would you say this influenced your becoming a deacon?
1. It was a primary influence......................... 10.4
2. It was a strong influence, but not primary. 25.8
3. It was some influence, but not very strong. 21.6
4. It was little to no influence. 22.1
5. Does not pertain................................ 20.0

Using the scale below, how would rate your relationship with the following?
[5] The bishop
1. I feel like a team member whose work is personally appreciated...................................... 30.2
2. I feel like a team member whose work is not known personally, but which is appreciated.................. 44.5

3. There is very little feeling of being a team member whose
work is appreciated. 12.4
4. There is no feeling of being a team member whose work is
appreciated. 9.9
5. Does not pertain.. . . . . 3.1

[6] Diocesan/religious priests I associate with in ministry
1. I feel like a team member whose work is personally
appreciated. 46.9
2. I feel like a team member whose work is not known
personally, but which is appreciated. 28.0
3. There is very little feeling of being a team member whose
work is appreciated. 16.5
4. There is no feeling of being a team member whose work is
appreciated 5.7
5. Does not pertain. 2.9

[7] Diocesan offices with whom I work
1. I feel like a team member whose work is personally
appreciated. 28.2
2. I feel like a team member whose work is not known
personally, but which is appreciated 28.6
3. There is very little feeling of being a team member whose
work is appreciated 13.6
4. There is no feeling of being a team member whose work is
appreciated. 8.4
5. Does not pertain 21.2

[8] My pastor
1. I feel like a team member whose work is personally
appreciated. 73.3
2. I feel like a team member whose work is not known
personally, but which is appreciated. 7.9
3. There is very little feeling of being a team member whose
work is appreciated 10.3
4. There is no feeling of being a team member whose work is
appreciated. 6.5
5. Does not pertain. 2.0

[9] My parish

1. I feel like a team member whose work is personally appreciated. 66.9
2. I feel like a team member whose work is not known personally, but which is appreciated. 23.1
3. There is very little feeling of being a team member whose work is appreciated. 4.9
4. There is no feeling of being a team member whose work is appreciated. 2.9
5. Does not pertain. 2.1

[10] My supervisor

1. I feel like a team member whose work is personally appreciated. 51.6
2. I feel like a team member whose work is not known personally, but which is appreciated. 7.6
3. There is very little feeling of being a team member whose work is appreciated. 4.9
4. There is no feeling of being a team member whose work is appreciated. 3.3
5. Does not pertain 32.6

[11] Other deacons with whom I work

1. I feel like a team member whose work is personally appreciated. 54.4
2. I feel like a team member whose work is not known personally, but which is appreciated. 23.2
3. There is very little feeling of being a team member whose work is appreciated. 6.2
4. There is no feeling of being a team member whose work is appreciated. 2.2
5. Does not pertain 14.0

[12] Lay parish staff
1. I feel like a team member whose work is personally
   appreciated. 56.2
2. I feel like a team member whose work is not known
   personally, but which is appreciated 22.1
3. There is very little feeling of being a team member whose
   work is appreciated. 9.4
4. There is no feeling of being a team member whose work is
   appreciated. 4.7
5. Does not pertain. 7.6

[13] My parish council
1. I feel like a team member whose work is personally
   appreciated. 43.1
2. I feel like a team member whose work is not known
   personally, but which is appreciated. 24.1
3. There is very little feeling of being a team member whose
   work is appreciated. 9.4
4. There is no feeling of being a team member whose work is
   appreciated. 6.6
5. Does not pertain 16.8

[14] Sisters with whom I work
1. I feel like a team member whose work is personally
   appreciated. 40.6
2. I feel like a team member whose work is not known
   personally, but which is appreciated. 12.7
3. There is very little feeling of being a team member whose
   work is appreciated. 6.1
4. There is no feeling of being a team member whose work is
   appreciated. 4.1
5. Does not pertain 36.5

[15] How would you describe your role?
1. There is a written role description, and it is followed 37.5
2. There is a written role description, but it is not followed. . . . 9.8
3. There is no written role description, just a mutual understanding, which works well 41.3
4. There is no written role description, just a mutual understanding, which does not work well. 6.0
5. Other arrangement(s) 5.4

Using the scale below, how would you rate the vision of the permanent diaconate by the following persons?

[16] The Bishop
1. There is a very clear vision of the role of the diaconate. 57.0
2. There is somewhat of an understanding of its role, but nothing very specific. 22.7
3. There is some confusion about its role. 7.4
4. There is much confusion about its role. 4.3
5. I don't really know. 8.1
6. Not applicable 0.4

[17] Diocesan priests I have met
1. There is a very clear vision of the role of the diaconate. 17.9
2. There is somewhat of an understanding of its role, but nothing very specific. 42.5
3. There is some confusion about its role. 27.5
4. There is much confusion about its role. 10.3
5. I don't really know 1.5
6. Not applicable. 0.2

[18] The pastor
1. There is a very clear vision of the role of the diaconate. 59.8
2. There is somewhat of an understanding of its role, but nothing very specific. 24.2
3. There is some confusion about its role. 7.9
4. There is much confusion about its role. 4.9
5. I don't really know 1.7
6. Not applicable 1.4

[19] My supervisor

1. There is a very clear vision of the role of the diaconate. 45.3
2. There is somewhat of an understanding of its role, but
   nothing very specific. 13.6
3. There is some confusion about its role. 3.8
4. There is much confusion about its role. 2.2
5. I don't really know 2.9
6. Not applicable. 32.0

[20] The parishioners

1. There is a very clear vision of the role of the diaconate. 13.6
2. There is somewhat of an understanding of its role, but
   nothing very specific. 42.6
3. There is some confusion about its role. 30.0
4. There is much confusion about its role. 10.9
5. I don't really know 2.0
6. Not applicable. 0.8

[21] Lay parish

1. There is a very clear vision of the role of the diaconate. 28.0
2. There is somewhat of an understanding of its role, but
   nothing very specific. 39.2
3. There is some confusion about its role. 17.3
4. There is much confusion about its role. 7.2
5. I don't really know 2.8
6. Not applicable 5.5

[22] My wife

1. There is a very clear vision of the role of the diaconate. 81.9
2. There is somewhat of an understanding of its role, but
   nothing very specific. 10.7
3. There is some confusion about its role. 1.9
4. There is much confusion about its role. 0.8
5. I don't really know. 0.6
6. Not applicable 4.1

[23] My children
1. There is a very clear vision of the role of the diaconate..... 53.4
2. There is somewhat of an understanding of its role, but
   nothing very specific............................. 29.4
3. There is some confusion about its role 7.0
4. There is much confusion about its role............... 1.4
5. I don't really know 2.0
6. Not applicable 6.8

[24] Diocesan permanent deacons
1. There is a very clear vision of the role of the diaconate..... 57.2
2. There is somewhat of an understanding of its role, but
   nothing very specific.............................24.7
3. There is some confusion about its role. 13.3
4. There is much confusion about its role. 2.5
5. I don't really know 1.7
6. Not applicable................................. 0.6

[25] The parish council
1. There is a very clear vision of the role of the diaconate..... 19.4
2. There is somewhat of an understanding of its role, but
   nothing very specific.............................37.6
3. There is some confusion about its role. 17.0
4. There is much confusion about its role. 6.5
5. I don't really know 6.6
6. Not applicable.................................12.9

[26] Sisters with whom I work
1. There is a very clear vision of the role of the diaconate..... 25.7
2. There is somewhat of an understanding of its role, but
   nothing very specific.............................22.5
3. There is some confusion about its role................. 8.6
4. There is much confusion about its role. 4.8
5. I don't really know................................. 5.5
6. Not applicable.................................32.8

[27] How often do you meet with parish staff to discuss your participation in parish ministry?
1. Almost weekly 18.1
2. Every few weeks 10.2
3. Monthly 18.7
4. Every few months 7.2
5. A few times in the year. 11.7
6. Almost never 28.6
7. Doesn't pertain, not in a parish 5.6

[28] Other than deacons with whom you work regularly, how often do you meet with other deacons to share ideas or pray together?
1. Almost always. 3.0
2. Every few weeks 4.2
3. Monthly 22.0
4. Every few months 23.8
5. A few times in the year. 31.2
6. Almost never 15.7

[29] How would you rate your sense of the needs of the diocese?
I discuss the needs of the diocese with persons who have knowledge of them:
1. To a large degree 16.7
2. To some degree 39.3
3. A little 17.0
4. Rarely 19.7
5. Never 7.3

[30] What more could be done to give you a better sense of the needs of the diocese?

[31] How well informed are you about diocesan meetings?
1. I receive regular announcements. 68.7
2. Communication about them is irregular. 17.4
3. I receive very little to no communication about them. 13.9

[32] How often do you attend diocesan meetings for deacons, when you are invited?

1. I almost always attend. 49.0
2. I attend with some frequency 25.3
3. I seldom attend 13.2
4. I almost never attend. 6.2
5. We never have diocesan meetings for deacons 6.3

[33] If you "seldom" or "almost never attend," why is this so? Please mark only those responses which pertain to you, and rank them with #1 being the first reason, #2 your second, etc.

Mean

1. I feel diocesan meetings generally do not speak to diaconal
   interests. 2.1
2. I have all I can do to attend local parish meetings. 2.0
3. Distance makes it very difficult to attend. 1.9
4. The timing of diocesan meetings does not coincide with the
   time available to me. 1.7
5. Other 1.7

[34] From the time you first began diaconal training to the day of ordination how long was your total preparation? (Please respond in years. Any time over a half of a year should be considered a full year. Any time below half of a year should not be counted.)

Mean

. . . . 3.5 years
. . . . sd. 1.026

[35] How would you evaluate the training you received in formation?

1. In all of my courses I felt I was being taught as if I were a
   young college student or seminarian 8.2
2. In a good number of my courses I felt I was being taught as
   a young college student or seminarian. 14.5
3. In a good number of courses I felt I was being taught as a
   grown adult with experience. 42.2
4. In all of my courses I felt I was being taught as a grown
   adult with experience. 35.1

Using the scale below, how would you evaluate the courses you received in formation?

[36] Ecclesiology
1. Excellent 32.7
2. Good. 44.0
3. Fair 15.5
4. Poor 2.4
5. Did not have a course in this 5.3

[37] Sacred Scripture
1. Excellent 54.8
2. Good. 34.0
3. Fair 8.7
4. Poor 1.9
5. Did not have a course in this 0.5

[38] Spiritual theology
1. Excellent 35.3
2. Good. 40.1
3. Fair 16.4
4. Poor 3.9
5. Did not have a course in this 4.3

[39] Liturgical theology
1. Excellent 29.5
2. Good. 34.8
3. Fair 22.1
4. Poor 8.1
5. Did not have a course in this 5.4

[40] Christology
1. Excellent 41.5
2. Good. 39.2
3. Fair 13.3
4. Poor 3.3
5. Did not have a course in this 2.7

[41] Moral theology
  1. Excellent 37.9
  2. Good 38.0
  3. Fair 16.3
  4. Poor 5.5
  5. Did not have a course in this 2.3

[42] Catechetics
  1. Excellent 21.2
  2. Good 37.5
  3. Fair 22.2
  4. Poor 6.3
  5. Did not have a course in this 12.9

[43] Church History
  1. Excellent 34.6
  2. Good 34.6
  3. Fair 17.8
  4. Poor 6.5
  5. Did not have a course in this 6.4

[44] Canon Law
  1. Excellent 25.9
  2. Good 31.6
  3. Fair 22.7
  4. Poor 10.9
  5. Did not have a course in this 8.6

[45] Homiletics
  1. Excellent 39.0
  2. Good 30.6
  3. Fair 18.3
  4. Poor 8.4
  5. Did not have a course in this 3.7

[46] Counseling
1. Excellent 21.4
2. Good 28.3
3. Fair 21.7
4. Poor 12.4
5. Did not have a course in this 16.2

[47] Vatican II documents
1. Excellent 23.0
2. Good 34.0
3. Fair 22.7
4. Poor 7.8
5. Did not have a course in this 12.5

[48] How well do you feel your talents are utilized in your ministry?
1. Used very much 61.5
2. Used somewhat 27.3
3. Used sparingly 8.5
4. Little to never used 2.7

[49] Using the scale below, in your formation how much emphasis was given to social ministries, like ministering to groups such as the physically impaired, the destitute, those of various cultures, etc.?
1. Very strong emphasis 12.8
2. Somewhat strong emphasis 20.1
3. Fair emphasis 30.3
4. Little emphasis 18.0
5. Very little emphasis 10.6
6. Never received any emphasis to my recollection 8.2

[50] How would you rate your formation in preparing you to use social referral agencies like Catholic Charities and Family Life Bureaus, etc.?
1. Excellent 8.5
2. Good 25.9
3. Fair 32.6
4. Poor 21.7
5. They were never addressed 11.3

[51] If married, did your wife participate in your formation?
1. Yes, she participated in all formation. 47.9
2. Yes, she participated in some formation. 28.1
3. Yes, but she participated in very little formation. 15.7
4. She did not participate in any of my formation. 5.6
5. Doesn't pertain. 2.8

[52] If you have children, how would you rate the effort made by the formation program to help them understand the diaconal ministry you were aspiring to?
1. Excellent 7.2
2. Good 18.9
3. Fair. 20.5
4. Poor 14.2
5. No effort was made 27.6
6. Does not pertain 11.7

[53] Did your formation program include seminarians training with you?
1. Yes. 6.1

[54] Did your formation program include lay persons training with you?
1. Yes 31.1

[55] If yes to either **#53** or **#54**, do you feel this was an asset to your training?
1. Yes 65.8
2. No 16.1
3. Not sure 18.1

[56] If no, do you feel persons training for other ministries would have been an asset?
1. Yes 23.2
2. No 34.3
3. Not sure 42.5

[57] How well do you feel your field training/internship prepared you?
1. Very well 26.5
2. Somewhat well 30.8
3. I am not sure 7.7
4. Somewhat poorly 6.2
5. Not at all 2.1
6. I did not have field training/internship 26.8

[58] Please comment on your response to **#57**.

[59] How much do you agree or not agree with the statement, Field training/internship should be more carefully chosen to better serve diocesan and community needs?
1. Strongly agree 53.9
2. Somewhat agree 28.2
3. Somewhat disagree 5.0
4. Strongly disagree 1.6
5. I don't know 11.3

[60] How often during the year do you attend seminars/lectures/discussion groups that address topics important for your ministry?
1. Almost weekly 2.4
2. Every few weeks 4.7
3. Monthly 9.3
4. Every few months 39.7
5. Once or twice a year 34.8
6. Almost never 10.0

[61] Please comment on your response to **#60**.

Besides the Bible, what one book in particular among the books you've read, do you consider especially important to your diaconal ministry?

[62] Title of book _____

[63] When did you read this book?
1. Before entering formation 14.9
2. During formation 33.9
3. After formation 38.6

[64] Have you incorporated any of the ideas in this book into your homilies?
1. Yes 79.8
2. No 8.6
3. Does not pertain, I don't give homilies 11.6

Using the scale below, how familiar are you with the following?
[65] *The Challenge of Peace*
1. Read it in its entirety 18.3
2. Read a good portion of it 10.9
3. Read some parts of it 12.3
4. Have not read it, but I am familiar with its contents through other resources 16.0
5. I am not familiar with this work 42.5

[66] *Economic Justice for All*
1. Read it in its entirety 22.2
2. Read a good portion of it 14.4
3. Read some parts of it 16.7
4. Have not read it, but I am familiar with its contents through other resources 17.4
5. I am not familiar with this work 29.4

[67] *The Consistent Ethic of Life*
1. Read it in its entirety 7.3
2. Read a good portion of it 6.6
3. Read some parts of it 9.3
4. Have not read it, but I am familiar with its contents through other resources 16.7
5. I am not familiar with this work 60.2

[68] *Sollicitudo Rei Socialis (On Social Concern)*
1. Read it in its entirety 6.9
2. Read a good portion of it 6.3
3. Read some parts of it 10.0
4. Have not read it, but I am familiar with its contents through other resources 16.4
5. I am not familiar with this work 60.4

[69] *Laborens Exercens (On Human Work)*
1. Read it in its entirety 12.2
2. Read a good portion of it 9.1
3. Read some parts of it 15.0
4. Have not read it, but I am familiar with its contents through
   other resources 20.3
5. I am not familiar with this work 43.4

[70] *Centesimus Annus (On the 100th Anniversary)*
1. Read it in its entirety 9.0
2. Read a good portion of it 6.4
3. Read some parts of it 9.1
4. Have not read it, but I am familiar with its contents through
   other resources 14.8
5. I am not familiar with this work 60.7

[71] *On Evangelization in the Modern World (Evangelii Nuntiandi)*
1. Read it in its entirety 28.3
2. Read a good portion of it 17.1
3. Read some parts of it 19.0
4. Have not read it, but I am familiar with its contents through
   other resources 14.9
5. I am not familiar with this work 20.6

[72] *Brothers and Sisters to Us*
1. Read it in its entirety 5.4
2. Read a good portion of it 4.2
3. Read some parts of it 5.7
4. Have not read it, but I am familiar with its contents through
   other resources 9.9
5. I am not familiar with this work 74.9

[73] *National Pastoral Plan for Hispanic Ministry*
1. Read it in its entirety 6.1
2. Read a good portion of it 3.8
3. Read some parts of it 4.4
4. Have not read it, but I am familiar with its contents through
   other resources 11.5
5. I am not familiar with this work 74.3

[74] *The Church and Racism: Towards a More Fraternal Society*
1. Read it in its entirety 5.1
2. Read a good portion of it 5.3
3. Read some parts of it 8.1
4. Have not read it, but I am familiar with its contents through
   other resources 19.2
5. I am not familiar with this work 62.3

[75] *On the Dignity and Vocation of Women*
1. Read it in its entirety 6.3
2. Read a good portion of it 6.8
3. Read some parts of it 10.8
4. Have not read it, but I am familiar with its contents through
   other resources 22.4
5. I am not familiar with this work 53.7

[76] *Redeemer of Man (Redemptor Hominis)*
1. Read it in its entirety 13.5
2. Read a good portion of it 9.3
3. Read some parts of it 15.3
4. Have not read it, but I am familiar with its contents through
   other resources 16.1
5. I am not familiar with this work 45.9

[77] *The Hispanic Presence*
1. Read it in its entirety 4.8
2. Read a good portion of it 2.8
3. Read some parts of it 3.5
4. Have not read it, but I am familiar with its contents through
   other resources 9.5
5. I am not familiar with this work 79.4

[78] *Here I Am, Send Me*
1. Read it in its entirety 12.9
2. Read a good portion of it 9.2
3. Read some parts of it 9.8
4. Have not read it, but I am familiar with its contents through
   other resources 12.6
5. I am not familiar with this work 55.4

[79] *What We Have Seen and Heard*
1. Read it in its entirety 7.5
2. Read a good portion of it 5.3
3. Read some parts of it 7.6
4. Have not read it, but I am familiar with its contents through
   other resources 9.5
5. I am not familiar with this work 70.0

[80] *Dogmatic Constitution on the Church*
1. Read it in its entirety 36.3
2. Read a good portion of it 22.0
3. Read some parts of it 18.9
4. Have not read it, but I am familiar with its contents through
   other resources 8.9
5. I am not familiar with this work 13.8

[81] *Dogmatic Constitution on Divine Revelation*
1. Read it in its entirety 32.1
2. Read a good portion of it 17.9
3. Read some parts of it 18.5
4. Have not read it, but I am familiar with its contents through
   other resources 10.6
5. I am not familiar with this work 20.8

[82] *Constitution on the Sacred Liturgy*
1. Read it in its entirety 41.2
2. Read a good portion of it 21.0
3. Read some parts of it 18.7
4. Have not read it, but I am familiar with its contents through
   other resources 9.4
5. I am not familiar with this work 9.8

[83] *Constitution on the Church in the Modern World*
1. Read it in its entirety 43.2
2. Read a good portion of it 19.9
3. Read some parts of it 17.6
4. Have not read it, but I am familiar with its contents through
   other resources 8.3
5. I am not familiar with this work 10.9

[84] *Decree on Ecumenism*
1. Read it in its entirety 31.7
2. Read a good portion of it 17.5
3. Read some parts of it 19.6
4. Have not read it, but I am familiar with its contents through
   other resources 13.6
5. I am not familiar with this work 17.5

[85] *Decree on the Bishops' Pastoral Office in the Church*
1. Read it in its entirety 18.2
2. Read a good portion of it 12.1
3. Read some parts of it 15.5
4. Have not read it, but I am familiar with its contents through
   other resources 18.6
5. I am not familiar with this work 35.7

[86] *Decree on Priestly Formation*
1. Read it in its entirety 15.1
2. Read a good portion of it 8.5
3. Read some parts of it 13.5
4. Have not read it, but I am familiar with its contents through
   other resources 20.1
5. I am not familiar with this work 42.7

[87] *Decree on the Apostolate of the Laity*
1. Read it in its entirety 28.9
2. Read a good portion of it 14.9
3. Read some parts of it 19.5
4. Have not read it, but I am familiar with its contents through
   other resources 15.7
5. I am not familiar with this work 20.9

[88] *Decree on the Ministry and Life of Priests*
1. Read it in its entirety 14.0
2. Read a good portion of it 7.1
3. Read some parts of it 13.3
4. Have not read it, but I am familiar with its contents through
   other resources 19.1
5. I am not familiar with this work 46.6

[89] *Decree on the Church's Missionary Activity*
1. Read it in its entirety 15.5
2. Read a good portion of it 9.0
3. Read some parts of it 14.0
4. Have not read it, but I am familiar with its contents through
   other resources 17.9
5. I am not familiar with this work 43.6

[90] *Declaration on Christian Education*
1. Read it in its entirety 16.2
2. Read a good portion of it 9.9
3. Read some parts of it 15.0
4. Have not read it, but I am familiar with its contents through
   other resources 17.7
5. I am not familiar with this work 41.3

[91] *Declaration on the Relationship of the Church to Non-Christian Religions*
1. Read it in its entirety 18.1
2. Read a good portion of it 9.6
3. Read some parts of it 13.4
4. Have not read it, but I am familiar with its contents through
   other resources 17.0
5. I am not familiar with this work 41.8

[92] *Declaration on Religious Freedom*
1. Read it in its entirety 18.8
2. Read a good portion of it 8.9
3. Read some parts of it 12.8
4. Have not read it, but I am familiar with its contents through
   other resources 17.0
5. I am not familiar with this work 42.5

Please check any of the documents which you have taught about, or used in a sermon.
[93] *The Challenge of Peace*
Yes 26.6

[94] *Economic Justice for All*
Yes 36.0

[95] *The Consistent Ethic of Life*
Yes 15.2

[96] *Sollicitudo Rei Socialis (On Social Concern)*
Yes 8.5

[97] *Laborens Exercens (On Human Work)*
Yes 15.6

[98] *Centesimus Annus (On the 100th Anniversary)*
Yes 7.7

[99] *On Evangelization in the Modern World (Evangelii Nuntiandi)*
Yes 39.9

[100] *Brothers and Sisters to Us*
Yes. 8.1

[101] *National Pastoral Plan for Hispanic Ministry*
Yes. 5.2

[102] *The Church and Racism: Towards a More Fraternal Society*
Yes 13.3

[103] *On the Dignity and Vocation of Women*
Yes 13.6

[104] *Redeemer of Man (Redemptor Hominis)*
Yes 16.4

[105] *The Hispanic Presence*
Yes. 5.6

[106] *Here I Am, Send Me*
Yes 20.9

[120] *Declaration on Religious Freedom*
Yes 14.3

Using the scale below, how would you rate your ministerial impact on the following?
[121] The workplace
1. Very strong impact. 22.6
2. Strong impact 29.5
3. Somewhat of an impact 31.3
4. Little impact 9.8
5. No impact to speak of 3.7
6. Never tried to impact on it 3.1

[122] Local government policies
1. Very strong impact 2.8
2. Strong impact 6.3
3. Somewhat of an impact 16.6
4. Little impact 25.0
5. No impact to speak of 22.9
6. Never tried to impact on it 26.3

[123] National government policies
1. Very strong impact 1.1
2. Strong impact 2.6
3. Somewhat of an impact 7.8
4. Little impact 21.0
5. No impact to speak of 32.0
6. Never tried to impact on it 35.6

[124] Advocacy or social change groups
1. Very strong impact 6.0
2. Strong impact 9.5
3. Somewhat of an impact 25.6
4. Little impact 18.8
5. No impact to speak of 17.0
6. Never tried to impact on it 23.0

If you make a "very strong" to "somewhat strong" impact, briefly describe on what, and how this is accomplished.

[125] On what do you impact?

[126] How do you impact?

[127] On what do you impact?

[128] How do you impact?

[129] On what do you impact?

[130] How do you impact?

[131] Are you responsible for guiding a small Christian community within your parish, or in particular sectors in society?
1. Yes 47.3

[132] Do you have any teaching responsibilities where you serve?
1. Yes 72.5

[133] If yes, what are the responsibilities?

[134] Have you been entrusted with pastoral care of a parish community that does not have a resident pastor?
1. Yes. 7.6

Using the scale below, how would you rate the efforts made to help you understand and deal with celibacy?
[135] During Formation
1. Very helpful 14.8
2. Somewhat helpful 19.8
3. Can't say 9.3
4. Of little help 15.5
5. Very unhelpful 2.4
6. No effort was ever made 38.2

[136] Now
1. Very helpful 12.7
2. Somewhat helpful 13.4
3. Can't say 11.3
4. Of little help 13.6
5. Very unhelpful 2.6
6. No effort was ever made 46.5

[137] If you were married and your wife died what would be your response toward mandatory celibacy?
1. I would accept celibacy as a gift from God 32.4
2. I would consider it an obligation based on tradition. 30.0
3. I would seek a dispensation from the diaconate to be free
   to marry. 7.1
4. I have not thought much about this. 19.2
5. Other 11.3

[138] How much time do you set aside to meditate each day?
1. 15 minutes or less 16.4
2. 15 minutes to a half hour. 32.6
3. A half hour to an hour 27.8
4. An hour or more 12.4
5. I don't meditate each day, but do it sporadically 10.9

[139] Outside the context of the Liturgy and Divine Office, how often do you set time aside to read the Bible?
1. Almost every day 28.2
2. Several times a week 26.9
3. About once a week 22.7
4. About twice a month. 6.7
5. About once a month 5.6
6. Once every few months or less 5.5
7. Almost never 5.3

[140] Other than those found in the Bible or Divine Office, how often do you read spiritual writers?
1. Almost every day 14.3
2. Several times a week 21.5
3. About once a week 20.7
4. About once a month 15.9
5. About twice a month 4.1
6. Once every few months or less 17.0
7. Almost never 6.5

[141] How often do you recite the rosary?
1. Almost every day 27.0
2. Several times a week 11.6
3. About once a week 13.9
4. About once a month 12.1
5. Once every few months or less 14.5
6. Almost never 21.1

[142] How frequently do you receive the sacrament of penance?
1. Almost on a weekly basis 3.8
2. On a monthly basis 14.2
3. Every couple of months 33.1
4. Once or twice a year 41.2
5. Almost never 7.7

[143] How important a role does the Divine Office play in your spiritual life?
1. It is the center of it 14.6
2. It plays a major role, but I wouldn't say it is the center of
   my spiritual life 35.0
3. It is important, but not major 29.5
4. It plays a minor to almost no role in my spiritual life 14.3
5. No role 6.6

Please prioritize in importance the experiences you have had that most energize your spiritual life with #1 being most important. Leave blank those experiences that do not pertain to you.

	Mean
[144] Prayer/meditation	2.6
[145] Retreats/days of renewal	4.1
[146] My spiritual director	4.8
[147] The spirituality of a person to whom I minister	4.8
[148] The Mass	2.2
[149] The sacrament of reconciliation	5.0
[150] Administering the sacraments	4.0
[151] Administering to the sick and dying	4.1
[152] Giving homilies	4.1
[153] My wife/family	2.8
[154] Other	3.7

[155] If you have one, please describe how often you meet with your spiritual director.
1. We meet once about every six months ... 9.8
2. We meet once about every three months ... 8.4
3. We meet once about every two months ... 8.4
4. We meet almost monthly ... 23.8
5. Do not have a spiritual director ... 49.6

[156] If you have a spiritual director, who is he or she?
1. Not applicable ... 27.0
2. A priest ... 52.3
3. Another deacon ... 5.8
4. A sister ... 7.7
5. A layman ... 1.3
6. A laywoman ... 3.0
7. Other ... 3.0

[157] If you have a spiritual director, to what extent does he/she enhance your ministry?
1. Not applicable 26.3
2. Very much 42.8
3. Somewhat 26.8
4. Very little 2.8
5. No effect 1.3

[158] How frequently do you make a retreat?
1. Once every few months 2.2
2. Twice a year 21.8
3. Once a year 65.9
4. Every few years 7.1
5. Almost never 3.0

[159] How frequently do you make days of recollection or renewal?
1. Almost weekly 8
2. Monthly 3.3
3. Every few months 16.3
4. About twice a year 30.7
5. Yearly 23.5
6. Almost never 25.3

[160] Is there a periodic evaluation of your diaconal ministry?
1. Yes 50.5

[161] If yes, is it
1. A written evaluation 57.6
2. An oral evaluation 35.6

[162] If evaluated, how helpful is it?
1. Very helpful 32.0
2. Somewhat helpful 46.6
3. Very little help 13.0
4. Almost no help 8.4

[163] If the evaluation is "very little" or "almost no help," what would you suggest to make it better?

[164] To what degree has being a deacon enhanced your family life?
1. I don't have a family 3.0
2. To a very great degree 30.9
3. To a large degree 36.8
4. Somewhat 17.8
5. To a small degree 4.0
6. No at all 1.4
7. I am not sure 3.8
8. It has hindered more than enhanced our family life 2.3

[165] To what degree has being a deacon enhanced your relationship with your wife?
1. I am not married 4.9
2. To a very great degree 34.4
3. To a large degree 31.8
4. Somewhat 15.5
5. To a small degree 4.7
6. Not at all 2.7
7. I am not sure 3.3
8. It has probably hindered more than enhanced our
   relationship 2.7

[166] To what degree has being a deacon enhanced your relationship with your children?
1. I do not have children 6.1
2. To a very great degree 19.4
3. To a large degree 29.1
4. Somewhat 25.0
5. To a small degree 8.7
6. Not at all 4.2
7. I am not sure 5.4
8. It has probably hindered more than enhanced our
   relationship 2.0

[167] What is your age as of your last birthday?

                                                              Mean
. . . . 59.5
. . . . sd 9.1

[168] In what year were you ordained a deacon?

Median

. . . . 1983

. . . . sd 6.0

[169] What has been the nature of your assignments?
1. Mostly assigned to my home parish 75.9
2. Mostly assigned to parishes in the diocese other than my own 7.7
3. Assigned to a diocesan position 2.0
4. I have a special assignment 4.0
5. Dually employed for my parish and the diocese 5.2
6. Other. 5.3

[170] How were you assigned?
1. By the bishop 59.8
2. By those in charge of the diaconate program 8.4
3. By personal choice. 24.8
4. Other 7.1

[171] In your opinion, what is the best way to be assigned to ministry?
1. By the bishop 42.8
2. By those in charge of the diaconate program. 10.9
3. By personal choice. 31.6
4. Other 14.7

[172] Did the diaconate training you received help you to fulfill the requirements of your assignment?
1. Definitely yes. 43.9
2. Yes 46.6
3. Very little 8.2
4. Definitely no. 1.3

[173] How much did your internship/field training prepare you in your assignments?

1. I did not have an internship/field training 36.4
2. It touched on many of the experiences I have experienced . . 26.4
3. It touched on some of the experiences I have experienced. . . 24.0
4. It touched on very little of the experiences I have
   experienced 6.8
5. It touched on almost none of the experiences I have
   experienced 3.5
6. I am not sure 2.8

[174] Before ordination did you have a specific idea about the type of assignment you wanted?

1. Yes 66.3

[175] If yes, have your expectations been fulfilled?

1. Yes, to a large extent 59.4
2. Yes, to some extent. 31.4
3. No, to a large extent 6.1
4. No, not at all 3.0

[176] After ordination, have your ideas about what assignment would be best for you changed?

1. Yes 31.7
2. No 58.7
3. Not sure. 9.6

[177] Would you recommend the diaconate to someone else?

1. Definitely yes. 69.2
2. Yes with reservations 29.5
3. Definitely no 1.3

[178] From your experience as a deacon, what would be the strongest reason for not recommending the diaconate? (If there are no reasons, write the word none.)

[179] From your experience, what would be the strongest reason for recommending the diaconate?

[180] What in your opinion is the biggest misconception about the diaconate?

[181] What is your marital status?
1. Married. 92.4
2. Single/never married 3.1
3. Separated 0.3
4. Divorced 1.1
5. Widowed 3.0

[182] If married, how many children are currently living at home?
Mean
. . . . .1.0
. . . . sd 1.2

[183] What is the highest level of education you have completed (excluding training for ministry)?
1. Less than high school 1.9
2. High school graduate or equivalent. 14.9
3. Some college 28.3
4. College graduate 15.2
5. Some graduate work 10.6
6. M.A./M.S. or equivalent 12.6
7. Post master's work 9.0
8. Ph.D. or equivalent. 7.4

[184] Are you bilingual?
1. Yes 22.3

[185] Which of the following categories corresponds to the type of community in which you presently live?
1. Farm (less than 5,000) 7.8
2. Village (5,001-10,000) 8.5
3. Town (10,001-20,000) 14.1
4. Small city (20,001-50,000). 17.5
5. Large city (50,000+) 34.5
6. Suburb of city 17.3
7. Military installation 0.1
8. Migrant community. 0.1

[186] Which of the following best describes the main racial or national background, and with which you identify?
1. English, Scottish, Welsh, English-Canadian 18.5
2. Irish 19.6
3. German, Austrian, Dutch, Swiss 15.2
4. Italian 8.2
5. French, French-Canadian, Belgian 3.9
6. Polish, Slovak, Lithuanian, Russian, Ukrainian, Hungarian . . 6.3
7. Other Eastern European, e.g., Czech, Slovenian, Croatian . . . 1.9
8. Hispanic, Mexican American, Puerto Rican, Central or South American 11.4
9. Portuguese 0.3
10. Asian, including Filipino 0.6
11. African American 3.8
12. African 0
13. Native American, American Indian 2.4
14. Other 8.0

[187] Which of the following categories best represents your occupation, or if retired, the occupation from which you retired?
1. Private household worker, laborer or service worker 1.8
2. Operative of machine (semi-skilled) 1.9
3. Foreman, craftsman, skilled worker 9.0
4. Clerical worker 2.7
5. Sales worker 4.8
6. Manager, official or proprietor 26.6
7. Professional (doctor, lawyer, teacher, etc.) 31.3
8. Farmer (laborer) 0.5
9. Farmer (manager) 0.6
10. Full-time employed as a deacon 6.8
11. Other 14.0

[188] Please give the name and address of your wife. (Check Not Applicable, if you don't have a wife.)
Not applicable 0.6

[189] Please give the name and address of your supervisor.

[190] Please give the name of your diocese.

[191] Please give the name and address of the person who is the president of your parish council.

[192] Do you plan to relocate out of the diocese within the next 5 years?
1. Definitely yes 2.5
2. Yes 3.7
3. No 63.8
4. Definitely no 15.3
5. Not sure 14.7

[193] What is your understanding of incardination? Please prioritize what comes to mind with #1 being your first idea of incardination.

	Mean
Being attached to a diocese	1.5
Being a servant of the Church	2.7
Being an extension of the bishop.	2.7
Focusing one's service in one place	3.9
Being assured of employment.	6.9
Being assured of sustenance in ministry	5.8
Being identified with a diocese	2.9
Having an obligation to inform the bishop of one's actions	4.3
Other	2.8

[194] Do you understand your obligation and rights as a cleric in accordance with the provisions of the 1983 *Code of Canon Law*?
1. Yes 79.6

[195] What did receiving the order of diaconate add to your life that was not in it before orders?

[196] Of all the experiences you have had as a deacon, what one was most dissatisfying?

[197] Of everything you have experienced in the permanent diaconate, what would you like to see improved?

[198] Do you believe dioceses should have a pension fund for permanent deacons?

    1. Yes 35.0

    2. No 27.8

    3. I am not sure. 37.2

[199] Please comment on your response.

[200] Do you believe dioceses should maintain a fund from which deacons could draw when faced with temporary financial emergencies?

    1. Yes 57.8

    2. No 16.6

    3. I am not sure. 25.5

[201] In what cases, if any, do you feel a permanent deacon should be compensated financially for his services?

[202] If you would like, please tell us what we should have asked but did not in this questionnaire.

A Study of Wives of Permanent Deacons
by The National Conference
of Catholic Bishops

1. What is your religious denomination?

	Percentages
1. Roman Catholic	98.1
2. Eastern Rite Catholic	0.2
3. Orthodox	.0
4. Protestant	1.2
5. Jewish	.0
6. Other	0.5

2. If you are a Catholic were you:

1. Born a Catholic	81.0
2. A convert	19.0

3. If you are a convert, when did you convert?

1. Before my husband's ordination	97.4
2. After my husband's ordination	2.6

4. Are you a member of any church-related organizations such as:
(Circle as many as apply.)

1. Council of Catholic Women	13.4
2. Parish Council	11.2
3. Sodality	8.1
4. Legion of Mary	4.0
5. Catholic Charismatic Renewal	14.0
6. Cursillo	27.0
7. Marriage Encounter	20.3
8. Other	39.9

5. Do you participate in any parish or diocesan ministries? (Circle as many as apply.)
   1. Lector 28.9
   2. Extraordinary eucharistic minister 55.0
   3. Catechist 21.2
   4. Visiting the sick or shut-ins 36.7
   5. Prison ministry 3.9
   6. Ministry to those of substance abuse 2.1
   7. Ministry to the poor or homeless 12.0
   8. Evangelization 10.4
   9. Rite of Christian Initiation of Adults (RCIA) 21.3
   10. Migrant/refugee ministry 1.5
   11. Battered women/children ministry 2.1
   12. Other 34.6

                                                                    Mean

6. What is your age as of your last birthday? 58.6

7. How many children do you have living at home? 1.0

8. If you have children, what is the age of your youngest child? . . 25.6

9. How many years have you been married to your husband? . . . 36.2

10. Which of the following best describes the main racial or national background?
   1. English, Scottish, Welsh, English-Canadian 16.4
   2. Irish 19.1
   3. German, Austrian, Dutch, Swiss 21.5
   4. Italian 10.8
   5. French, French-Canadian, Belgian 5.6
   6. Polish, Slovak, Lithuanian, Russian, Ukrainian, Hungarian . . 6.8
   7. Other Eastern European, e.g., Czech, Slovenian, Croatian . . 1.6
   8. Hispanic, Mexican American, Puerto Rican, Central or
      South American 4.2
   9. Portuguese 0.1
   10. Asian, including Filipino 1.2
   11. African American 3.0
   12. Native American 9.1

11. What is the highest level of education you have completed?
    1. Less than high school 3.4
    2. High school graduate or equivalent. 35.0
    3. Some college 32.4
    4. College graduate 13.5
    5. Some graduate work. 5.5
    6. M.A./M.S. or equivalent 6.0
    7. Post master's work 3.4
    8. Ph.D. or equivalent 0.8

12. Are you bilingual?
    1. Yes 12.3

Using the scale below, how often do you participate in the following?
13. Participate in the arts, e.g., go to concerts, visit museums, etc.
    1. Once a week. 1.8
    2. Once a month or more. 11.8
    3. A few times a year 74.2
    4. Never 12.1

14. Participate in continuing education courses
    1. Once a week. 4.4
    2. Once a month or more 8.8
    3. A few times a year 66.9
    4. Never 19.9

15. Participate in spiritual renewal opportunities such as retreats/days
of reflection
    1. Once a week. 1.4
    2. Once a month or more 6.4
    3. A few times a year 85.0
    4. Never. 7.1

16. Are you presently employed outside the home and earning a salary?
    1. Yes 48.8

17. If yes, how would you describe this work?
    1. Part-time 37.7
    2. Full-time. 62.3

18. If yes to question 16, how would you describe the type of work you do?

19. Beside employment, are you involved in other activities on a regular basis such as volunteer work, being a student, etc.
   1. Yes 62.3

20. If you answered yes to question 19, how deeply involved are you?
   1. Quite involved 44.2
   2. Involved 50.4
   3. Rarely involved 3.8
   4. Never involved 1.7

21. If you consider yourself to be "Quite involved" or "Involved" in your husband's ministry how would you describe this involvement?

22. Do you have a formal ministry which is distinct from that of your husband's?
   1. Yes 43.7

23. If yes, how would you describe this ministry?

24. Did you participate in your husband's preparation for the diaconate?
   1. Yes 93.6

25. If yes, please check those areas in which you participated.
   1. Attended all or almost all formal sessions 66.2
   2. Attended some formal sessions 21.9
   3. Attended sessions designed especially for deacons' wives . . . 10.1
   4. Made days of spiritual renewal and retreat. 1.8

26. How did you feel about the length of time in which you participated in your husband's formation?
   1. I did not participate in his formation 5.5
   2. It was just the right amount of time 79.2
   3. It should have been less time. 3.9
   4. It should have been more time 11.4

27. In what year was your husband ordained? 1983

28. In your experience, how would you rate your husband's program of formation?
    1. Excellent 39.6
    2. Good. 50.9
    3. Fair 7.0
    4. Poor 1.0
    5. Don't know 1.5

29. In your experience, what changes would you suggest in the formation program for the wives of deacons?

30. Regarding your husband's decision to pursue ordination to the diaconate, would you say:
    1. I was very supportive and encouraging from the beginning . 75.2
    2. I was supportive but retained some reservations 21.6
    3. I was neutral with regard to his decision 2.1
    4. I was not very supportive of his decision 0.6
    5. I was antagonistic with regard to his decision 0.4
    6. I really can't say 0.1

31. Prior to your husband's ordination, how would you rate your involvement in church related activities?
    1. Quite involved 46.0
    2. Involved 40.7
    3. Rarely involved 11.4
    4. Never involved 1.9

32. Since your husband's ordination, how would you rate your personal involvement in church related activities?
    1. Quite involved 39.9
    2. Involved 44.1
    3. Rarely involved 13.8
    4. Never involved 2.2

33. Since your husband's ordination, have you thought or reacted negatively to his ministry?
    1. Yes 20.9

34. If yes, do you react negatively to:
    1. Your husband's specific ministry 12.1
    2. The diaconate in general 22.2
    3. Something other (describe) 65.7

35. How would you describe your own spiritual growth:
    1. Growing significantly 43.3
    2. Growing slowly 37.3
    3. About the same 16.9
    4. Drying up 2.5

In terms of receiving affirmation from others, please rank the following persons or groups of persons by means of the following categories:
36. Your children
    1. Very affirming 47.6
    2. Affirming 37.7
    3. Neutral 13.2
    4. Non-affirming 1.0
    5. I don't know 0.5

37. Your husband
    1. Very affirming 73.9
    2. Affirming 21.4
    3. Neutral 3.5
    4. Non-affirming 0.4
    5. I don't know 0.7

38. Your pastor
    1. Very affirming 35.2
    2. Affirming 35.2
    3. Neutral 16.3
    4. Non-affirming 7.8
    5. I don't know 5.4

39. Other priests
  1. Very affirming 20.0
  2. Affirming 45.4
  3. Neutral 19.9
  4. Non-affirming 5.8
  5. I don't know 9.0

40. Religious sisters
  1. Very affirming 26.7
  2. Affirming 38.3
  3. Neutral 14.0
  4. Non-affirming 4.8
  5. I don't know 16.1

41. Long-time friends
  1. Very affirming 39.9
  2. Affirming 44.7
  3. Neutral 13.0
  4. Non-affirming 0.5
  5. I don't know 1.9

42. The bishop
  1. Very affirming 30.7
  2. Affirming 29.3
  3. Neutral 13.3
  4. Non-affirming 6.0
  5. I don't know 20.7

43. Other deacons
  1. Very affirming 46.5
  2. Affirming 40.3
  3. Neutral 6.9
  4. Non-affirming 0.6
  5. I don't know 5.7

44. Other deacons' wives
    1. Very affirming 44.0
    2. Affirming 39.5
    3. Neutral 9.1
    4. Non-affirming 1.2
    5. I don't know 6.1

45. Neighbors
    1. Very affirming 15.3
    2. Affirming 33.1
    3. Neutral 29.8
    4. Non-affirming 2.3
    5. I don't know 19.5

46. Others (Please describe.)
    1. Very affirming 33.2
    2. Affirming 27.9
    3. Neutral 14.6
    4. Non-affirming 3.4
    5. I don't know 20.8

Using the scale below how strongly do you agree or disagree with the following?
47. I feel a sense of pride that my husband is an ordained minister.
    1. Strongly agree 67.2
    2. Agree 28.3
    3. Disagree 9
    4. Strongly disagree 2
    5. I really can't say 2.0
    6. Doesn't apply 1.4

48. The priests my husband works with see him as a valuable colleague.
    1. Strongly agree 39.7
    2. Agree 40.8
    3. Disagree 8.8
    4. Strongly disagree 3.6
    5. I really can't say 6.3
    6. Doesn't apply 8

49. Sometimes I feel that some priests resent working with a married deacon.
1. Strongly agree 19.6
2. Agree. 47.1
3. Disagree 12.8
4. Strongly disagree 4.0
5. I really can't say 14.0
6. Doesn't apply 2.5

50. In general, the time I spend with my husband and family is very fulfilling.
1. Strongly agree 66.3
2. Agree. 31.3
3. Disagree. 1.0
4. Strongly disagree. 2
5. I really can't say 7
6. Doesn't apply 4

51. I feel that my husband has the personal qualities required for diaconal ministry.
1. Strongly agree 80.4
2. Agree. 18.1
3. Disagree 3
4. Strongly disagree. 1
5. I really can't say 9
6. Doesn't apply 1

52. Since my husband's ordination, I feel I no longer have enough time to pursue my own interests.
1. Strongly agree 1.3
2. Agree 3.5
3. Disagree 52.9
4. Strongly disagree 35.8
5. I really can't say 1.2
6. Doesn't apply 5.2

53. I actively share in my husband's ministry.
   1. Strongly agree 21.8
   2. Agree. 45.6
   3. Disagree 18.9
   4. Strongly disagree 2.7
   5. I really can't say 2.7
   6. Doesn't apply 8.2

54. The diaconate has had a positive effect on the way my husband and I relate to each other.
   1. Strongly agree 31.6
   2. Agree. 47.5
   3. Disagree. 5.9
   4. Strongly disagree 1.2
   5. I really can't say 8.1
   6. Doesn't apply 5.7

55. Most of the priests we know truly respect my husband because of his personal talents.
   1. Strongly agree 37.6
   2. Agree. 47.1
   3. Disagree. 5.1
   4. Strongly disagree 1.2
   5. I really can't say 9.0
   6. Doesn't apply 0

56. I think some deacons use their ministry as an excuse for not dealing with family problems.
   1. Strongly agree 6.1
   2. Agree. 20.3
   3. Disagree 16.8
   4. Strongly disagree 8.2
   5. I really can't say 46.3
   6. Doesn't apply 2.3

57. My husband sometimes uses his ministry as an excuse for not dealing with family problems.
1. Strongly agree 1.5
2. Agree 5.7
3. Disagree 39.2
4. Strongly disagree 47.1
5. I really can't say 2.9
6. Doesn't apply 3.6

58. I feel the parish expects too much of me because of my husband's position as a deacon.
1. Strongly agree 1.7
2. Agree 4.4
3. Disagree 53.7
4. Strongly disagree 26.8
5. I really can't say 7.1
6. Doesn't apply 6.3

59. Since studying theology, my husband thinks he knows all there is about the faith.
1. Strongly agree 1.4
2. Agree 2.6
3. Disagree 43.7
4. Strongly disagree 48.6
5. I really can't say 1.3
6. Doesn't apply 2.5

60. I feel that the priests in our parish have a difficult time relating to me as the wife of an ordained minister.
1. Strongly agree 4.7
2. Agree 7.7
3. Disagree 53.0
4. Strongly disagree 23.2
5. I really can't say 8.1
6. Doesn't apply 3.3

61. Since ordination, my husband's interest in his own secular career or occupation has diminished.
1. Strongly agree 3.5
2. Agree. 10.1
3. Disagree 44.6
4. Strongly disagree 26.7
5. I really can't say 1.5
6. Doesn't apply 13.6

62. My husband's ordination has had little or no impact on the way I choose to spend my time.
1. Strongly agree 10.9
2. Agree. 41.7
3. Disagree 35.7
4. Strongly disagree 7.8
5. I really can't say 1.2
6. Doesn't apply. 2.8

63. Because of his ordination, I feel that my husband is often used and taken advantage of.
1. Strongly agree 5.3
2. Agree. 17.3
3. Disagree 55.9
4. Strongly disagree 15.8
5. I really can't say 4.4
6. Doesn't apply. 1.2

64. Since ordination, my husband sometimes has a "holier than thou" attitude about himself.
1. Strongly agree 1.2
2. Agree 4.8
3. Disagree 44.0
4. Strongly disagree 47.5
5. I really can't say 1.0
6. Doesn't apply. 1.6

65. Because of ordination, it seems we have less time as a couple "to get away from it all" and simply relax.
1. Strongly agree 5.5
2. Agree. 21.2
3. Disagree 48.0
4. Strongly disagree 22.1
5. I really can't say 7
6. Doesn't apply 2.5

66. I sometimes feel that I am in competition with the Church for my husband's love and affection.
1. Strongly agree 2.9
2. Agree 9.1
3. Disagree 46.4
4. Strongly disagree 38.8
5. I really can't say 7
6. Doesn't apply 2.1

67. I sometimes feel that the persons my husband serves treat him as a mere worker rather than a committed minister.
1. Strongly agree 4.1
2. Agree. 21.3
3. Disagree 46.7
4. Strongly disagree 22.0
5. I really can't say 4.5
6. Doesn't apply 1.4

68. I sometimes think most laity do not really understand that deacons are not "priest-assistants," but ordained clergy in our Church.
1. Strongly agree 27.3
2. Agree. 48.0
3. Disagree 14.7
4. Strongly disagree 3.1
5. I really can't say 6.3
6. Doesn't apply 6

69. My husband often puts his ministerial responsibilities ahead of his family responsibilities.
1. Strongly agree 2.2
2. Agree. 12.5
3. Disagree 54.0
4. Strongly disagree 28.4
5. I really can't say 1.1
6. Doesn't apply 1.7

70. I sometimes think that my husband should devote the time and energy he gives to the diaconate to his own secular career or occupational advancement.
1. Strongly agree 4
2. Agree 3.7
3. Disagree 49.7
4. Strongly disagree 29.0
5. I really can't say 1.5
6. Doesn't apply 15.6

71. In general, deacons spend an equivalent amount of time with their families as do other working men.
1. Strongly agree 5.4
2. Agree. 43.1
3. Disagree 21.6
4. Strongly disagree 4.6
5. I really can't say 24.3
6. Doesn't apply 1.0

72. In general, I feel that my husband really wishes he had pursued ordination to the priesthood.
1. Strongly agree 2.3
2. Agree 5.5
3. Disagree 48.5
4. Strongly disagree 35.1
5. I really can't say 6.9
6. Doesn't apply 1.7

73. Because of my husband's ordination, my own understanding of the Church's mission has increased.
1. Strongly agree 25.2
2. Agree. 55.0
3. Disagree 12.6
4. Strongly disagree 2.3
5. I really can't say 3.3
6. Doesn't apply 1.6

74. As a result of my husband's ordination, my friends are not as open in our relationship.
1. Strongly agree 1.6
2. Agree 6.9
3. Disagree 58.9
4. Strongly disagree 26.9
5. I really can't say 3.9
6. Doesn't apply 1.8

75. Since ordination, my husband tends to expect too much from the people to whom he ministers.
1. Strongly agree 1.3
2. Agree 2.6
3. Disagree 56.1
4. Strongly disagree 35.1
5. I really can't say 3.6
6. Doesn't apply 1.3

76. What has being the wife of a deacon meant to you?

77. In what ways, if any, are your husband's expectations of you influenced by the fact he is a deacon?

78. During your husband's ordination you heard him promise the bishop obedience and respect. What was your reaction to this?
1. It seems right with me 86.0
2. I wondered how that would affect our marriage 6.6
3. I wondered how that would affect our family 4.1
4. I had negative feelings. 3.3

79. If there are children in your family, what effect, if any, has your husband's diaconate had on their home life?

80. Do you find that there is more or less love expressed between the two of you because of your husband becoming a deacon?

81. Since your husband became a deacon, do you feel the freedom to pursue your own religious practice in your own way?
   1. Yes, entirely 72.3
   2. Yes, to a great degree 20.4
   3. I feel little less free 5.1
   4. I feel a lot less free 7
   5. I really can't say 1.6

82. What would you suggest to a woman whose husband was thinking of becoming a deacon?

Paragraph 72 of the diaconal guidelines reads: "The wives and families of married candidates should be involved in the various aspects of the formation program. Relationships among deacons and their wives and children are bound to be affected by the new commitments that deacons make. These changes will be handled much more easily if the wives and at least the older children gain an understanding and appreciation of the new ministry that their husbands and fathers will be undertaking and of how it will affect them. Diaconal commitments and family relationships will thus enrich and confirm one another."

83. Does your experience correspond to the guidelines?
   1. Yes 82.7
   2. No. 7.8
   3. I am not sure 9.5

84. If no, what would you add?

85. If you knew then what you know now, would you have given your consent to your husband's ordination to the order of deacon?
   1. Yes 92.4
   2. No. 1.1
   3. I am not sure 6.4

86. Have you ever felt the need for a support group to better understand your husband's ministry?
   1. Yes 33.3

87. Do you believe dioceses should help to take care of a deacon when
he gets sick?
   1. Yes 45.8
   2. No 18.1
   3. I am not sure. 36.1

88. How do you feel about deacons not being able to remarry if
widowed?

89. How has your husband becoming a deacon effected your spiritual
life?

90. Is there anything important that we forgot to ask that you would
like to share?

National Conference of Catholic Bishops Diaconate Study for Supervisors and Directors of Deacons

1. What is your vocational status?
   1. Lay person. 9
   2. Religious brother 2
   3. Religious sister. 3.6
   4. Permanent deacon. 6.5
   5. Priest 88.0
   6. Bishop 8

2. In the diaconate program, what does your role involve:
   1. Director of diocesan program for deacons 8.5
   2. Supervisor of deacon interns who are in formation 6.9
   3. Long-term supervisor of deacons 47.3
   4. Other 37.3

3. Overall how committed is your diocese to the process of supervising, providing counseling and giving direction to permanent deacons?
   1. It is very committed. 54.3
   2. Somewhat committed 35.0
   3. It is not very committed. 8.4
   4. It is not committed at all 2.3

4. If you feel it is little or not committed, what do you believe is needed to change this?

5. Have you had formal training which might have prepared you for your role?
   1. Yes 42.4

6. Please evaluate the training you received for your role.
   1. Very satisfactory. 20.6
   2. Satisfactory 31.8
   3. Unsatisfactory 2.2
   4. Very unsatisfactory 9
   5. I received no training. 44.4

7. If you received satisfactory training, briefly describe it.

8. Please estimate the total number of hours you spent preparing for your role. Check none if there was no preparation.
　None . . . . [46.7% of respondents]
　Average hours for those who had preparation 63.8

9. In light of your experience, how was the time you spent preparing for role?
　1. Very adequate 30.1
　2. Somewhat adequate 22.0
　3. Somewhat inadequate 5.2
　4. Very inadequate. 2.6
　5. I had no preparation 40.0

10. Who appointed you to your role?
　1. Bishop. 53.9
　2. Diocesan personnel board. 1.9
　3. Pastor 2.5
　4. Director of permanent diaconate program. 10.3
　5. Myself. 19.2
　6. Other 12.2

11. How many years have you been in this role?

Average Yrs.
. . . . 8.6

12. If you had a choice, would you continue in this role?
　1. Yes 86.8
　2. No 5.2
　3. Don't know 8.0

13. Please briefly explain why you would or would not continue.

14. Which of the following statements characterizes how you understand your responsibilities?
1. There is a written role description, and it is followed. 40.5
2. There is a written role description, but it is not followed. . . . 2.8
3. There is no written role description, just a mutual understanding, which works well. 48.7
4. There is no written role description, just a mutual understanding, which does not work well. 5.8
5. Other 2.2

15. If there is a written role description, who wrote it?
1. Bishop. 10.7
2. Diocesan personnel board. 4.4
3. Pastor 7.5
4. Director of permanent program 42.9
5. Myself. 15.5
6. Other 19.0

16. Does the role description still accurately describe your actual responsibilities?
1. Yes 39.7

17. In general, what is your personal reaction to the restoration of the permanent diaconate?
1. Very positive 65.3
2. Somewhat positive. 28.8
3. Somewhat negative 4.8
4. Very negative. 8
5. I really can't say 4

18. What two pieces of literature have been most helpful to you in your role as supervisor? Check none, if no literature helped you.
Found nothing helpful 47.6

19. Could the ministries that your deacon(s) perform be performed equally well by a lay person (or this same person) without ordination?
    1. No, definitely not 32.3
    2. No, probably not 23.2
    3. Maybe. 15.3
    4. Yes, probably by most of the deacons 20.3
    5. Yes, definitely could be done by a lay person. 8.9

20. The diocesan bishop in general is supportive of the permanent diaconate.
    1. Strongly agree. 5.7

21. Diocesan priests are supportive of the permanent diaconate.
    1. Strongly agree. 7.6
    2. Agree. 70.4
    3. Disagree 13.5
    4. Strongly disagree. 2.1
    5. I don't know 6.5

22. Parishioners understand the role of deacons for the most part.
    1. Strongly agree. 7.8
    2. Agree. 62.2
    3. Disagree 23.4
    4. Strongly disagree. 3.8
    5. I don't know 2.7

23. Priests have grown more supportive of the diaconate than they were years ago.
    1. Strongly agree. 17.6
    2. Agree. 62.1
    3. Disagree 9.7
    4. Strongly disagree. 1.7
    5. I don't know 8.9

24. Parishioners have come to understand the role of deacon better than years ago.
    1. Strongly agree 18.0
    2. Agree. 67.6
    3. Disagree 10.2
    4. Strongly disagree 1.1
    5. I don't know 3.0

25. Sisters have come to appreciate the role of deacon.
    1. Strongly agree 8.0
    2. Agree. 33.8
    3. Disagree 16.2
    4. Strongly disagree 4.9
    5. I don't know 37.1

26. Parish staffs have come to appreciate the role of deacon.
    1. Strongly agree 22.2
    2. Agree. 61.0
    3. Disagree 8.4
    4. Strongly disagree 1.0
    5. I don't know 7.4

27. The permanent diaconate is needed more now than when it was when first restored.
    1. Strongly agree 41.5
    2. Agree. 37.9
    3. Disagree 8.8
    4. Strongly disagree 2.9
    5. I don't know 9.0

28. The diaconate will grow substantially in numbers in the next five years in our diocese.
    1. Strongly agree 15.8
    2. Agree. 31.1
    3. Disagree 18.1
    4. Strongly disagree 4.8
    5. I don't know 30.2

29. Granted this varies from parish to parish, overall, how well are most of the deacons introduced to the community they serve?
   1. Very well for most of the deacons I supervise 48.1
   2. Somewhat well 44.2
   3. Not well 5.9
   4. Almost never happens 1.4
   5. It is nonexistent 4

Using the scale below each group, how much ongoing instruction and updating on the role of the permanent diaconate is happening with the following groups?
30. Parishioners
   1. It is happening on a very regular basis. 6.1
   2. It is happening on a somewhat regular basis. 20.1
   3. It is somewhat irregular. 35.4
   4. It is very irregular. 19.3
   5. It is almost to totally nonexistent. 16.0
   6. I really don't know. 3.1

31. Priests
   1. It is happening on a very regular basis. 6.3
   2. It is happening on a somewhat regular basis. 25.3
   3. It is somewhat irregular. 31.6
   4. It is very irregular. 17.2
   5. It is almost to totally nonexistent. 14.4
   6. I really don't know. 5.1

32. Religious
   1. It is happening on a very regular basis. 3.6
   2. It is happening on a somewhat regular basis. 15.7
   3. It is somewhat irregular. 20.5
   4. It is very irregular. 11.3
   5. It is almost to totally nonexistent. 14.7
   6. I really don't know. 34.2

33. Bishop(s)
    1. It is happening on a very regular basis. 16.5
    2. It is happening on a somewhat regular basis. 13.4
    3. It is somewhat irregular. 10.0
    4. It is very irregular. 2.8
    5. It is almost to totally nonexistent. 4.5
    6. I really don't know. 52.8

34. Parish staffs
    1. It is happening on a very regular basis. 8.1
    2. It is happening on a somewhat regular basis. 24.2
    3. It is somewhat irregular. 32.5
    4. It is very irregular. 15.0
    5. It is almost to totally nonexistent. 12.8
    6. I really don't know. 7.5

35. Do deacons with whom you work have a written delineation of
their responsibilities?
    1. Yes 78.6

36. Do you think deacons need a written delineation of their
responsibilities?
    1. Yes 88.0

37. In general, how would you describe the relationship between most
deacons' wives and the priests with whom they minister?
    1. Very warm and respectful. 47.8
    2. Somewhat warm and respectful 35.5
    3. Somewhat distant 8.2
    4. Very distant 8
    5. I really can't say 6.6
    6. Does not pertain 1.1

38. In general, how much collaboration do you see between deacons and their pastors?
    1. Very much collaboration. 39.4
    2. Some collaboration 51.5
    3. Very little collaboration 6.3
    4. No collaboration. 6
    5. I don't know 2.3

39. In general, how much satisfaction or dissatisfaction is expressed over this collaboration?
    1. Very much satisfaction 26.4
    2. Some satisfaction. 38.8
    3. Some dissatisfaction. 20.8
    4. Great dissatisfaction. 3.6
    5. I don't know 10.3

40. In general, how much collaboration do you see between deacons and parish staff?
    1. Very much collaboration. 31.1
    2. Some collaboration 52.3
    3. Very little collaboration. 10.5
    4. No collaboration 1.5
    5. I don't know 4.6

41. In general, how much satisfaction or dissatisfaction is expressed over this collaboration?
    1. Very much satisfaction 22.5
    2. Some satisfaction. 40.3
    3. Some dissatisfaction. 21.9
    4. Great dissatisfaction. 2.3
    5. I don't know 13.1

42. In general, how much do you see deacons and priests collaborating as a team?
    1. To a great degree. 31.8
    2. To a fair degree 54.1
    3. Very little. 12.9
    4. To almost no degree. 1.2

43. How many deacons are you presently directing or supervising?
Average no. of deacons 2.7
I don't direct or counsel on a long-term basis.

If you do not direct or counsel on a long-term basis go to question 73.

44. What do you consider to be an appropriate number of deacons to work with?
Average no. of deacons. 3.5

45. How did you and the deacons you supervise decide on how often you should meet to discuss the deacon's ministry?
1. This was part of my written role description. 14.2
2. This was understood by the time of ordination. 2.9
3. This was suggested by the bishop. 4.7
4. This was suggested by the pastor. 3.4
5. My suggestion 18.7
6. Supervisee's suggestion 1.6
7. We both decided this was a good schedule. 43.0
8. I don't recall. 11.3

46. Does your diocese have guidelines about how frequently supervisors and deacons should meet?
1. Yes 28.5
2. No 39.8
3. I don't know 31.7

47. In general, do you find the frequency of your meetings with the deacons you direct and counsel?
1. About right 71.1
2. Not often enough. 27.3
3. Too many 1.5

48. Over time, have you found the frequency of your meetings with the deacon(s) you supervise:
1. Increasing 19.3
2. Decreasing. 19.8
3. About the same 60.7

49. What are the three most common concerns you discuss with the deacons you direct and counsel?

If you are presently directing and counseling more than one deacon, please think of the overall general impression they give when you answer the following questions.

50. In general, how frequently do you generally discuss the deacon's ministry with him?
1. Weekly 17.3
2. Monthly 30.8
3. Every few months 30.8
4. Yearly 14.3
5. Rarely or never 6.9

51. How would you broadly characterize your relationship with the deacon(s) you direct and counsel?
1. Nodding acquaintance 1.6
2. Persons who are engaged in separate areas of ministry, but are aware and interested in each other's work when time permits 26.7
3. Senior colleague–junior colleague in deciding together what kinds of ministerial work needs to be done, allocating the work between us, and giving each other supportive critique in accomplishing it 35.7
4. Captain–First Mate: I assign deacon(s) work in line with his or their capabilities and interests and discuss the progress of the deacon(s)' work regularly, giving the deacon(s)' supportive critique 20.0
5. Expert–Novice: I assign the deacon(s) work I feel needs to be done and that he or they can do with some supervision, supervise the deacon(s)' work fairly closely on a regular basis. 2.4
6. Other 13.6

52. Do you believe that the deacon(s) you direct and counsel would devote the same time to his/their present ministry if not ordained?
1. No, definitely would not without ordination 26.9
2. No, probably not 38.4
3. Maybe, would not, maybe would 15.9
4. Yes, probably 15.9
5. Yes, definitely would be as willing without ordination 2.9

53. Did you know the deacon(s) you direct and counsel before he/they became a candidate for the permanent diaconate?
   1. Yes, most of them. 24.5
   2. Yes, a few of them 60.1
   3. No, none of them. 15.4

54. If yes, did you personally encourage this man/men to pursue ordination to the diaconate?
   1. Yes, most of them. 44.5
   2. Yes, a few of them 46.0
   3. No, none of them. 9.5

*Using the scale below, how would you rate the overall effectiveness of **most** deacon(s) you direct and counsel in the following?*
55. Preparing and giving homilies
   1. Very effective 35.6
   2. Somewhat effective 50.5
   3. Ineffective 6.2
   4. Deacon does not perform this ministry 6.7
   5. I really don't know. 1.0

56. Religious education
   1. Very effective 29.5
   2. Somewhat effective 50.4
   3. Ineffective 3.7
   4. Deacon does not perform this ministry 13.6
   5. I really don't know. 2.9

57. Participation in parish/diocesan administration
   1. Very effective 19.9
   2. Somewhat effective 40.1
   3. Ineffective 6.0
   4. Deacon does not perform this ministry 31.2
   5. I really don't know. 2.9

58. With the poor
   1. Very effective 33.8
   2. Somewhat effective 37.7
   3. Ineffective 3.9
   4. Deacon does not perform this ministry 18.6
   5. I really don't know. 6.0

59. Pro-life movement
   1. Very effective 20.2
   2. Somewhat effective 37.5
   3. Ineffective 4.3
   4. Deacon does not perform this ministry 30.1
   5. I really don't know. 8.0

60. Prison ministry
   1. Very effective 18.2
   2. Somewhat effective 14.4
   3. Ineffective 4.3
   4. Deacon does not perform this ministry 52.8
   5. I really don't know. 9.8

61. Work with small base communities
   1. Very effective 13.6
   2. Somewhat effective 22.8
   3. Ineffective 5.8
   4. Deacon does not perform this ministry 50.0
   5. I really don't know. 7.5

62. Visiting sick/elderly
   1. Very effective 53.6
   2. Somewhat effective 34.9
   3. Ineffective 2.3
   4. Deacon does not perform this ministry 7.8
   5. I really don't know. 1.3

63. Promoting human and civil rights
    1. Very effective 15.3
    2. Somewhat effective 37.6
    3. Ineffective 7.0
    4. Deacon does not perform this ministry 30.6
    5. I really don't know. 9.4

64. Sacramental activities e.g., baptisms, marriages, liturgies
    1. Very effective 58.4
    2. Somewhat effective 36.4
    3. Ineffective 2.1
    4. Deacon does not perform this ministry 2.1
    5. I really don't know. 1.0

65. Counseling
    1. Very effective 21.4
    2. Somewhat effective 40.2
    3. Ineffective 5.6
    4. Deacon does not perform this ministry 24.9
    5. I really don't know. 7.9

66. Rite of Christian Initiation (RCIA), inquiry classes
    1. Very effective 38.5
    2. Somewhat effective 30.9
    3. Ineffective 3.7
    4. Deacon does not perform this ministry 24.0
    5. I really don't know. 2.9

67. Leader of prayer groups, charismatics, marriage encounter
    1. Very effective 33.8
    2. Somewhat effective 24.5
    3. Ineffective 4.5
    4. Deacon does not perform this ministry 33.5
    5. I really don't know. 3.4

68. Evangelization
    1. Very effective 21.5
    2. Somewhat effective 45.2
    3. Ineffective 5.3
    4. Deacon does not perform this ministry 22.1
    5. I really don't know. 5.9

69. Preach, teach, or inform others about the social teaching of the
Catholic Church
    1. Very effective 21.0
    2. Somewhat effective 46.5
    3. Ineffective 8.2
    4. Deacon does not perform this ministry 18.1
    5. I really don't know. 6.1

*Please describe any other diaconal ministries that may have been
overlooked and rate them.*
70. Ministry_____

71. Ministry_____

72. Ministry_____

73. Since its restoration, has the ministry of the diaconate turned out as
    you expected?
    1. Very much so. 15.5
    2. Pretty much so 54.0
    3. I don't know 11.8
    4. Not quite. 15.9
    5. Much different. 2.9

74. If you answered, not quite or much different please tell us in what
way(s).

75. Do you feel the diaconal formation programs with which you are familar are adequate?
    1. Yes, very satisfactory 18.7
    2. Yes, satisfactory 48.9
    3. No, not satisfactory 19.1
    4. No, very dissatisfactory 5.0
    5. I really don't know. 8.3

76. If no, please list the 3 most evident areas of dificiency.

77. How effective do you believe your role has been?
    1. Very effective 20.6
    2. Somewhat effective 64.1
    3. Not very effective. 8.3
    4. Ineffective 1.7
    5. I don't know 5.2

78. If you answered *not very* or *almost ineffective*, please tell us why.

79. How much do you use the *1984 Guidelines on the Permanent Diaconate* which were published by the National Conference of Catholic Bishops?
    1. Very often 9.5
    2. Somewhat often. 19.5
    3. Seldom 29.5
    4. Almost never 14.7
    5. I haven't read these guidelines 26.8

80. To whom do you give an accounting of your supervision or direction/counseling of deacons?
    1. To no one 37.3
    2. To the bishop. 21.3
    3. To the pastor. 1.5
    4. To the personnel board 1.0
    5. To the director of the diaconate program 35.4
    6. Other (Describe) 3.5

81. Please briefly describe how (e.g., oral, written, scheduled, annually, etc.) you give this accounting.

82. In general, how well do you feel deacons are trained to work with other leadership groups in the parish?
    1. Very well 15.8
    2. Fairly well 51.1
    3. Somewhat poorly 20.0
    4. Very poorly 4.4
    5. I really don't know 8.7

83. What do you believe are the two most satisfying experiences deacons have?

84. What direction(s) do you think the permanent diaconate will take in, say, the next decade?

85. What direction(s) would you like to see it take?

86. In terms of the direction(s) you'd like the diaconate to take, what are the impediments you see to this?

87. What added spiritual dimensions do deacons bring to the Church that weren't there before the diaconate?

88. All things being equal, in general, whom do you think would make the best director for deacons?
    1. Priests 33.7
    2. Bishops 2.5
    3. Religious brothers 2
    4. Religious sisters 4
    5. Lay persons 1.8
    6. Permanent deacons 41.3
    7. Can't say 14.9
    8. Other (describe) 5.3

89. All things being equal, in general, whom do you think would make the best supervisor/counselor for deacons?
   1. Priests 44.0
   2. Bishops 1.4
   3. Religious brothers 4
   4. Religious sisters 4
   5. Lay persons 1.4
   6. Permanent deacons 31.0
   7. Can't say 14.9
   8. Other (describe) 6.5

90. Please briefly describe your choice.

91. Deacons promise not to marry if they become widowed. From your experience, do you think their formation programs adequately teach the meaning of this rule?
   1. Very adequately 16.9
   2. Adequately 29.9
   3. Don't know 36.8
   4. Inadequately 10.2
   5. Very inadequately 6.1

92. Deacons sometimes speak of an "identity problem." Is this generally true in your experience?
   1. Yes 42.0

93. If *yes*, what are the major reasons for this?

94. Does your role ever bring you into contact with the deacon's family and wife?
   1. Not applicable 1.1
   2. Never 8
   3. Rarely 8.8
   4. Sometimes 32.6
   5. Often 56.8

95. In your experience, have the deacons' ministerial duties ever conflicted with their family obligations?
   1. Does not apply 1.9
   2. Often 9.5
   3. Sometimes. 6.8
   4. Rarely. 48.7
   5. Never 33.1

96. Have you ever been asked to counsel a deacon's wife?
   1. Never 67.8
   2. Once or twice 17.1
   3. A few times 13.7
   4. Often 1.3

97. Have you ever been asked to counsel a deacon and his wife?
   1. Never 76.2
   2. Once or twice 14.4
   3. A few times 8.4
   4. Often 1.0

98. What is your age of as your last birthday?
   Average age. 54.3

99. How would you describe the work which occupies the largest portion of your weekly schedule, e.g., teaching, parish work, hospital or social work?

100. If you work within a parish structure, which of the following best describes your position?
   1. Pastor 87.9
   2. Associate pastor 2.5
   3. Parish staff member. 3.1
   4. Other (describe) 6.6

101. If you are a priest, permanent deacon or member of a religious community, for how many years have you been ordained or professed? Check if none of these.
   Average years 27.1

102. What is the highest academic degree you have achieved?
1. Less than college degree. 2.5
2. B.A., S.T.B., or other bachelor's 20.9
3. M.A. S.T.L., M.DIV., M.S., or other master's 64.8
4. Doctorate 11.7

103. What is your predominant racial/ethnic background?
1. African American 2
2. Caucasian 93.7
3. Hispanic 1.7
4. Native American 1.9
5. Asian 6
6. Other (describe) 1.9

104. Is there any question you think should have been asked about the supervision of deacons, but wasn't?

APPENDIX C

. . . .

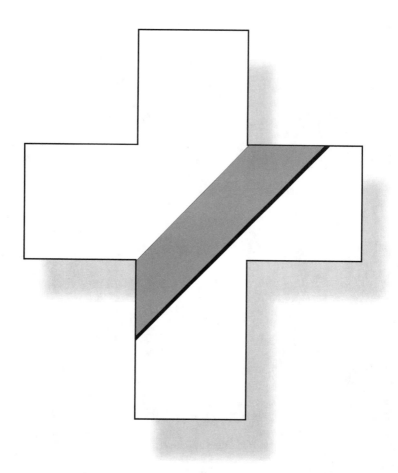

A National Study of the Permanent Diaconate
Sampling Procedure

Table 5 reflects the percentage of returns on the four phases of the national study of permanent deacons.

TABLE 5

	Sent out	Returned	%
Deacons	9,000	5,369	60%
Wives	1,850	1,194	64%
Supervisors	1,719	533	31%
Parish Councils	1,716	600	33%

Rationale Behind the Diaconate Sampling

In Phase I, we received 5,369 returns. It is impractical to process all 5,369 returns when a good random sample gives the same results, therefore 3,073 questionnaires were randomly picked from the 5,369 returns. The margin of error for Phase 1 is no more than 3 +/– percentage points.

To ensure that African Americans, Hispanics, Asians, Native Americans, Eskimos, and Aleuts were represented, any deacon in the 5,369 returns found to be of these cultures was included. Hence, within the random sample, there is a selected sample of cultures other than white Anglos.

Phases II, III, and IV drew their sample from addresses the deacons in Phase I gave for their wives, supervisors, and parish councils.

In Figure 3, we have a nationwide picture of the actual number of questionnaires that were returned from each diocese. It should be noted that dioceses that reflect no deacon returns do so either because they don't have the permanent diaconate (twenty-seven such dioceses exist), or because they did not send in the names of their deacons. Also, a diocese may not be represented because it has few deacons and the sampling missed them. Or it could be that the deacon removed the name of the diocese on the returned questionnaire, making the diocese anonymous.

FIGURE 3

NUMBER OF RESPONSES
FROM EACH (ARCH)DIOCESE

30	Albany (N.Y.)	02	Crookston (Minn.)
01	Alexandria (La.)	35	Dallas (Texas)
06	Altoona-Johnstown (Pa.)	22	Davenport (Iowa)
13	Amarillo (Texas)	11	Des Moines (Iowa)
07	Anchorage (Alaska)	39	Detroit (Mich.)
27	Arlington (Va.)	24	Dubuque (Iowa)
34	Atlanta (Ga.)	07	Duluth (Minn.)
14	Austin (Texas)	10	Evansville (Ind.)
44	Baltimore (Md.)	01	Fairbanks (Alaska)
04	Baton Rouge (La.)	09	Fargo (N.D.)
10	Beaumont (Texas)	13	Fort Wayne-South Bend (Ind.)
05	Belleville (Ill.)		
06	Biloxi (Miss.)	25	Fort Worth (Texas)
05	Birmingham (Ala.)	61	Galveston-Houston (Texas)
06	Bismarck (N.D.)	14	Gary (Ind.)
62	Boston (Mass.)	02	Great Falls (Mont.)
23	Bridgeport (Conn.)	26	Green Bay (Wis.)
30	Brooklyn (N.Y.)	18	Harrisburg (Pa.)
22	Brownsville (Texas)	80	Hartford (Conn.)
25	Buffalo (N.Y.)	10	Helena (Mont.)
08	Burlington (Vt.)	09	Honolulu (Hawaii)
29	Camden (N.J.)	11	Houma-Thibodaux (La.)
22	Charleston (S.C.)	08	Jackson (Miss.)
18	Charlotte (N.C.)	18	Jefferson City (Mo.)
167	Chicago (Ill.)	37	Joliet (Ill.)
56	Cincinnati (Ohio)	02	Juneau (Alaska)
41	Cleveland (Ohio)	01	Kalamazoo (Mich.)
05	Colorado Springs (Colo.)	22	Kansas City-St. Joseph (Mo.)
16	Columbus (Ohio)		
08	Covington (Ky.)	04	Knoxville (Tenn.)

06	La Crosse (Wis.)	08	St. Cloud (Minn.)
24	Lafayette (La.)	59	St. Louis (Mo.)
23	Lansing (Mich.)	06	St. Maron of Brooklyn
10	Las Cruces (N.M.)	55	St. Paul and Minneapolis
14	Little Rock (Ark.)		(Minn.)
39	Los Angeles (Calif.)	18	St. Petersburg (Fla.)
21	Louisville (Ky.)	17	Salt Lake City (Utah)
09	Manchester (N.H.)	10	San Angelo (Texas)
04	Marquette (Mich.)	59	San Antonio (Texas)
35	Miami (Fla.)	22	San Bernadino (Calif.)
47	Milwaukee (Wis.)	31	San Diego (Calif.)
60	New Orleans (La.)	04	San Jose in California
65	New York (N.Y.)	58	Santa Fe (N.M.)
37	Newark (N.J.)	11	Scranton (Pa.)
12	Norwich (Conn.)	39	Seattle (Wash.)
19	Oakland (Calif.)	13	Sioux City (Iowa)
20	Ogdensburg (N.Y.)	06	Sioux Falls (S.D.)
15	Oklahoma City (Okla.)	14	Spokane (Wash.)
35	Omaha (Neb.)	14	Springfield in
14	Orange in California		Massachusetts
32	Paterson (N.J.)	02	Steubenville (Ohio)
27	Pensacola-Tallahassee	10	Stockton (Calif.)
	(Fla.)	16	Superior (Wis.)
33	Peoria (Ill.)	22	Syracuse (N.Y.)
31	Philadelphia (Pa.)	51	Toledo (Ohio)
49	Phoenix (Ariz.)	49	Trenton (N.J.)
09	Pittsburgh (Pa.)	09	Tulsa (Okla.)
06	Portland in Oregon	07	Tyler (Texas)
16	Providence (R.I.)	13	Venice (Fla.)
10	Rapid City (S.D.)	38	Victoria in Texas
32	Rochester (N.Y.)	55	Washington (D.C.)
30	Rockford (Ill.)	10	Wheeling-Charles. (W.Va.)
57	Rockville Centre (N.Y.)	14	Wilmington (Del.)
30	Sacramento (Calif.)	23	Worcester (Mass.)
10	Saginaw (Mich.)	06	Yakima (Wash.)
09	St. Augustine (Fla.)	17	Youngstown (Ohio)

BIBLIOGRAPHIC RESOURCES

Documentation

Catechism of the Catholic Church, English-Language Translation for the United States. Washington, D.C.: United States Catholic Conference, 1994.

Committee on the Permanent Diaconate, National Conference of Catholic Bishops. *Permanent Deacons in the United States: Guidelines on Their Formation and Ministry*, 1984 Revision. Washington, D.C.: United States Catholic Conference, 1985.

Congregation for Divine Worship. *General Instruction of the Roman Missal*, English Translation of the Fourth Edition (1975). Washington, D.C.: United States Catholic Conference, 1982.

Paul VI. Apostolic letter, in *motu proprio* form, *Ad Pascendum (Laying Down Certain Norms Regarding the Sacred Order of the Diaconate)*. Washington, D.C.: United States Catholic Conference, 1972.

_____. Apostolic letter, in *motu proprio* form, *Sacrum Diaconatus Ordinem (General Norms for Restoring the Permanent Diaconate in the Latin Church)*. Washington, D.C.: United States Catholic Conference, 1967.

Recommended Reading List

The following books may prove useful to candidates for the diaconate, to deacons, and to diocesan program directors.

Barnett, James M. *The Diaconate, A Full and Equal Order*. New York: The Seabury Press, 1981.

Brockman, Norbert, S. M. *Ordained to Service: A Theology of the Permanent Diaconate*. Hicksville, N.Y.: Exposition Press, 1976.

Canon Law Society of America, *The Canonical Implications of Ordaining Women to the Permanent Diaconate*. Washington, D.C.: CLSA, 1995.

Collins, John. *Diakonia: Re-interpreting the Ancient Sources.* New York: Oxford University Press, 1990.

Deacon Digest. Green Bay, Wis.: Alt Publishing Company.

Echlin, Edward P. *The Deacon in the Church: Past and Future.* New York: Alba House, 1971.

Gregorios, Paulos Mar. *The Meaning and Nature of Diakonia.* Geneva, Switzerland: WCC Publications, 1988.

van Klinken, Jaap. *Diakonia: Mutual Helping with Justice and Compassion.* Grand Rapids, Mich.: William B. Eerdmans Publishing Company, 1989.

Kraus, Theodore W. "The Order of Deacon Revisited," Touchstone, Vol. XI, No. 3 (Spring 1996).

Kwatera, Michael. *The Liturgical Ministry of Deacons.* Collegeville, Minn.: The Liturgical Press, 1985.

Landregan, Steve. *Speak Lord! Reflections on the Ordination Rite for Deacons.* Washington, D.C.: United States Catholic Conference, 1987.

Martimort, A. G. *Deaconesses: An Historical Study.* San Francisco: Ignatius Press, 1986.

McCaslin, Patrick and Michael G. Lawler. *Sacrament of Service.* New York: Paulist Press, 1986.

National Conference of Catholic Bishops, Committee on the Permanent Diaconate, *Foundations for the Renewal of the Diaconate.* Washington, D.C.: United States Catholic Conference, 1993

_____ , Committee on the Liturgy. Bishops. *Study Text III: Ministries in the Church.* Washington, D.C.: United States Catholic Conference, 1974.

_____ . *Study Text VI: The Deacon Minister of Word and Sacrament.* Washington, D.C.: United States Catholic Conference, 1996.

Olson, Jeannie E. *One Ministry Many Roles: Deacons and Deaconesses Through the Centuries.* St. Louis: Concordia Publishing House, 1992.

Osborne, Kenan B. *The Diaconate in the Christian Church: Its History and Theology—A Look at the Past and A Dream for the Future.* Cleveland: Archangel Crusade of Love, 1996.

Shaw, Russell. *Permanent Deacons.* Third Edition. Washington, D.C.: United States Catholic Conference, 1995.

Sherman, Lynn C. *The Deacon in the Church.* New York: Alba House, 1991.

Shugrue, Timothy J. *Service Ministry of the Deacon.* Washington, D.C.: United States Catholic Conference, 1988.